DISRUPT DISRUPTION

DISRUPT
DISRUPTION

How to Decode the Future,
Disrupt Your Industry, and
Transform Your Business

Pascal Finette

NEW DEGREE PRESS

COPYRIGHT © 2023 PASCAL FINETTE

DISRUPT DISRUPTION

How to Decode the Future, Disrupt Your Industry, and Transform Your Business

ISBN   979-8-88504-451-6 *Paperback*

          979-8-88504-493-6 *Hardcover*

          979-8-88504-475-2 *Ebook*

To the rebels, troublemakers, and radicals—build what matters.

Contents

If you're going through hell, keep going.

—WINSTON CHURCHILL

Foreword

I remember the night Pascal and I met. I had gone to yet another industry event, as I often did in those days, when I was introduced to a tall, lanky, energetic fellow with a French-sounding name and a German-sounding accent. At the time, he worked for Google, but with his restless energy, I could tell the sleepy corporate life—no matter how remarkable the company—was not his destiny.

That random, serendipitous meeting turned into a decade-long friendship. We kept running into each other, like when we discovered we were both mentoring social entrepreneurs for the Unreasonable Group and spent a convivial evening in Boulder, Colorado, sipping a fine bourbon and sharing our enthusiasm for working with amazing innovators. Eventually, we even took our show on the road speaking to audiences together, since our chosen topics—disruption and *blitzscaling*—fit so well together (including in the pages of this book!).

Blitzscaling, which refers to the pursuit of rapid growth by prioritizing speed over efficiency in the face of uncertainty, is a powerful force that has helped build companies like Apple, Amazon, and Airbnb but can only succeed under a very specific set of circumstances. The goal of blitzscaling is to win a valuable winner-take-most market; this kind of opportunity only presents itself in either a new or newly transformed market.

In other words, disruption is the necessary precondition of blitzscaling.

As such, any entrepreneur, intrapreneur, or CEO who wants to win big has to develop a keen eye for spotting a disruption-driven opportunity earlier than the competition and a strong stomach for the relentless blitzscaling it takes to become an enduring market leader in a new multibillion- or multitrillion-dollar industry.

Until now, however, spotting disruption has been more of an art than a science. The late great Clayton Christensen was the first to define disruptive innovation by observing that disruptive technologies seem inferior to incumbents initially, then gradually catch up and surpass them. This pattern doesn't always make it easy to spot disruption. After all, many new, inferior technologies exist! The vast majority of such developments are destined to quickly fade into obscurity, and trying to blitzscale any opportunities they create makes setting a pile of money on fire seem like fiduciary responsibility.

What we've needed is a practical set of guidelines for discovering today what will matter tomorrow.

This book can do that for you. In page after page and chapter after chapter, Pascal dives deep into the many different facets of disruption, its antecedents and consequences, and how it can impact you and your business. In some cases, you'll read about the iconic stories of disruption, such as the iPhone, but Pascal breathes new life into these stories with novel and insightful perspectives and details others ignore or gloss over. In other cases, you'll read the story of one of the many actual practitioners Pascal has worked with to identify disruption and, even more importantly, bring it to market successfully.

And in every chapter, Pascal provides a point-by-point summary of the most important takeaways and insights. You'll want to buy a paper copy just so you can dog-ear each of his tl;drs!

Beyond the content, which is excellent, you'll also hear Pascal's inimitable voice on every page—thoughtful, helpful, and excited about what's to come. If you want to imagine and create the future, you've found your perfect guide.

Chris Yeh

Coauthor of the bestselling book *Blitzscaling: The Lightning-Fast Path to Building Massively Valuable Companies* and general partner at Blitzscaling Ventures

November 2022

Mind the Gap

If we want things to stay as they are, things will have to change.
—GIUSEPPE TOMASI DI LAMPEDUSA, THE LEOPARD

Thirty years ago, on an unusually sunny spring day outside Berlin, Germany, a much younger version of myself sat in my fire-red, beaten-up Toyota sedan, eyes fixed on two high piles of foam boxes. My task was straightforward: don't hit the boxes. I was instructed to accelerate fast and hit the brakes hard once the wheels of my car made contact with a large plastic tarp drenched in water. All I needed to do was not hit the boxes while the vehicle slid across the tarp. I hit the boxes five times in a row.

I would have hit the now disheveled pile of boxes a sixth time if it wasn't for the instructor of the drivers' safety training I was attending. Instead of fixing my gaze on the obstacle I was trying to avoid, she urged me to stare at the gap I was trying to get through. Lo and behold, it worked.

Observe anyone whose job is to navigate obstacles—from Formula One drivers to wild-water kayakers to container ship captains making their way into port—and how they focus solely on the gap, never the obstacle.

The same is true for our quest to decipher and become better at innovation, disruption, and transformation. Too often, we fixate on the obstacle rather than the gap. This book shows you how to find and successfully navigate the gap—the difficult but discernible path a leader must find to navigate transformation's (sometimes lethal) challenges. You will learn to decode the future, disrupt your industry, and transform your business.

DISRUPTING DISRUPTION

Disruption is everywhere—and nowhere more so than in the business world. You can't open a news website, browse through a magazine, or read a LinkedIn post without someone proclaiming (loudly) yet another case of "disruption." Industries and businesses get disrupted, disruptors are hailed as modern-day gladiators, and the disrupted are being dragged into the limelight for one last laugh before they are forgotten for good. I used to work for a leading executive education organization in the heart of Silicon Valley, the land of milk and honey when it comes to disruption; I am certainly guilty as charged for my fair share of overusing the word "disruption."

Our world today is shaped by the exponentially accelerating forces of technology. From computers, artificial intelligence, and robotics to the dramatic advances we are making in life sciences and beyond, not a single industry isn't going through rapid change. Mix in a highly complex and constantly shifting geopolitical landscape and abruptly changing consumer preferences, and you have all the ingredients for a perfect storm. Weathering, navigating, and thriving in the rough waters coming with this storm require us to unlearn many of the leadership skills that served us so well in times of relative calm and stability and lean into a new set of skills.

Understanding disruption, preparing us and our businesses for the future, and learning to ride the tidal waves of change has become a—if not *the*—leadership skill needed today.

Yet, as the old saying goes, we miss the forest for the trees. We read, talk, and think about innovation, disruption, and transformation—and get lost in the deep, dark woods of TBU: true but useless. The canon of literature that makes us nod in agreement and simultaneously scratch our heads with questions on what to do with this information is vast. It ranges from advice to be more "agile" without much explaining what this is supposed to mean in practical terms to a whole article series in a well-respected business publication on "being human at work." Add to this the other side of the coin—academic papers and the books written on top of those, trying to capture an inherently dynamic and messy reality in mathematical formulas and flowcharts—and you find yourself no better off: book intelligent but not street smart.

Too much of the advice and insight given either borders on platitudes or doesn't hold up when you try to implement it. Operators regularly fail to apply fancy theories and models when working on the front lines of disruptive change.

I experienced this firsthand when teaching the ins and outs of disruption at the executive education organization mentioned above. I have worked for some of the most innovative and disruptive companies of their time—eBay, Mozilla Firefox, and Google—building my businesses in the space; taught masterclasses at the world's best schools, including London Business School, ESMT Berlin, Switzerland's IMD, Berkeley Haas, and Stanford University; and advised Fortune 500 companies and SMBs all around the world on the topic. As someone who has spent his whole career in the trenches of disruptive change, I got utterly frustrated with the lack of a clear, down-to-earth, proven guide to managing it successfully. So, I decided to write one.

In the course of this work, I interviewed more than 250 world-leading practitioners—people who have successfully transformed companies and industries. I asked them a straightforward question. I wasn't interested in the theory or the strategy; all I wanted to know was: What are you doing? In other words: How do you fix your gaze on the gap?

The result of four years of in-depth study, cross-referenced with the literature on innovation, disruption, and transformation—all tested and refined with the clients of be radical, the consulting firm I cofounded—forms the basis for this book.

If you are involved with an innovation endeavor, tasked with disrupting your industry or the old way your company does things, or part of a transformation initiative, this book is for you. The insights, tools, and frameworks will serve you well regardless of role, level, or function. Throughout our voyage, you will learn to read the tea leaves which make up our future, gain a different perspective on disruption, explore the four most common faults of transformation initiatives, and discover the five keys to unlocking disruptive change in your organization. This book will help you with the beginning, middle, and end of your journey—a journey which, I might add, will never end.

In his 1905 play *Man and Superman*, Irish playwright George Bernard Shaw pointed out "the reasonable man adapts himself to the world; the unreasonable one persists in trying to adapt the world to himself. Therefore, all progress depends on the unreasonable man" (Shaw 1962).

Let's be unreasonable, put the pedal to the metal, and focus on the gap.

PART ONE
DECODE

1
Decoding the Future

I am interested in the future because I expect to spend the rest of my life in the future.

—CHARLES E. KETTERING

"The past is a foreign country. They do things differently there." The immortal first line of British novelist and short story writer L. P. Hartley's book *The Go-Between* (2015) wistfully condenses the problems inherent to memory and history. In the same way the past feels like a foreign country, so does the future—presenting itself in the form of a thick, seemingly impenetrable fog.

On our journey to manage disruptive change successfully, we start by decoding the future. We skillfully surf the tsunami waves brought about by ever-faster emerging innovations and the changes these create. As distant as the past and future might feel, we can learn from them. Learning from the past is common practice (think about sports practice where we try, fail, learn, rehearse, or the (in)famous Lean Startup methodology (Ries 2011), which brought the same approach to the world of business). Doing so with regard to our future is equally as valuable. Our first order of business will be to peer into the fog, detect the earliest indicators of change long before they turn into trends, and carefully evaluate what we find to ensure we are on the right path.

But before we get there, let's talk about the future at large.

In his book *The Art of the Long View: Planning for the Future in an Uncertain World*, the futurist Peter Schwartz coined the term "the official future" (2012). Your official future is the set assumption of how the future will play out—for you, your family, your community, and your company. It is the story a company tells itself about how things will be—which type of business it will be in, what the growth rate will be, and how much money it will make by selling its products and services. The future is, by definition, unknowable. There isn't just one "official" possible way the future will play out, but a nearly *unlimited* number of possible futures. The scope of possible futures widens the further out into the future you look: from economic and political to social factors. The bigger the distance between the here and now to the future becomes, the less able you will be to determine their direction and strength—creating uncertainties compounding into an ever-growing array of possible futures.

Your "official future" is inherently limited—a vision for a singular future based on a single set of assumptions and insights. The invitation—no, the obligation—for the future leader is to "kill the official future" (Crews 2015) and embrace the spectrum of possible futures. In the process, you will find and chart your course toward your preferred future.

You don't have *a* future.

You have *many* futures.

1.1
The Future Is ...

It is very difficult to predict, especially the future.

—*NIELS BOHR*

The year is 1993. *The X-Files* made its television debut and showed us, once and for all, "the truth is out there." That same year Marc Andreessen, now one of the world's most successful venture capital investors, and Unix expert Eric Bina released NCSA Mosaic, the first proper web browser (Computer History Museum n.d.). Intel released the Pentium chip, Apple the Newton handheld computer, and era-defining technology magazine *Wired*'s first issue hit the newsstand, proclaiming "the digital revolution is whipping through our lives like a Bengali typhoon" (WIRED 2018).

This was also the year US telecom giant AT&T tasked documentary filmmaker David Hoffman with producing a promotional video showcasing its vision for the future of computing. Their vision outlined "an electronic community where people can easily and inexpensively communicate, get and share information, learn, play, shop" using cutely animated pencil drawings. AT&T called this service "PersonaLink" and explained, "you can think of our electronic meeting place as *the cloud*" (Hoffman 2013).

If that term sounds familiar ... it took a good ten years between AT&T coining the term in its PersonaLink video and Amazon's launch of Amazon Web Services (AWS) in mid-2002 to make us think about computer servers in data centers and not white fluffy shapes in the sky when we hear the word "cloud." Search for the word cloud on your internet search engine of choice. The top results are all for cloud computing services, not the "collection of visible vapor, or watery particles, suspended in the upper atmosphere" (Miriam-Webster n.d.).

The same happened to other terms, which received a whole new meaning due to the way technology took over: your handle has become your online identifier (used to present yourself to millions of other users around the world), not the part of an instrument you hold in your bare hands (and later the often colorful nicknames truck drivers gave each other on CB radio). Trolls have turned from supernatural beings to nasty humans harassing folks on the internet, and a tweet used to be the sound a little bird makes.

Ten years can feel long and short at the same time. It's the gap between AT&T showcasing their innovation and this innovation turning profoundly disruptive. Disruption, which could have been spotted early, took a decade to materialize.

But AT&T didn't stop there: over the course of six minutes and forty-seven seconds, the video describes online social networks (years before Friendster, Myspace, and now Facebook), mobile phone-based navigation (it took until 2007 for Google Maps to debut), and intelligent agents—a concept which now goes by the acronym RPA ("Robotic Process Automation," one of the hottest things in the business community these days). It took at least an entire decade before any of these concepts became mainstream.

Wired magazine's founding executive editor and technology visionary par excellence Kevin Kelly points out chapter after chapter in his book *The Inevitable* (2017): when it comes to technology, the future has already happened. We are just catching up. Technology, indeed, has become inevitable.

THE FUTURE IS A PARADOX

"The future is …"—how would you complete this sentence? What word comes to mind first? Bright? Now? Uncertain? Scary? Maybe your answer has shifted as you've grown older—from pure, untarnished excitement when thinking about the future the moment you left college to a grimmer outlook after watching Al Gore's 2006 climate change documentary *An Inconvenient Truth*? Or maybe it sways daily, depending on the headlines?

Before we begin to decode the future, we ought to check in with ourselves—our assumptions, perspectives, and biases toward the future. Over the years, my colleagues at be radical and I have posed this question to tens of thousands of people globally, ranging from high schoolers to Fortune 500 CEOs. The responses are all over the spectrum—from crazy optimism to fatalistic pessimism. They are all correct. Each answer is the right one; the future is all of these responses at the same time.

Considering our future, we often face uncertainty, ambiguity, concerns, and fears. Think about the climate crisis or the political situation in many countries around the world. Yet, numerous moments in our daily lives present the future in a bright, hopeful light (as parents will attest when they look into the eyes of their newborn child and see limitless opportunity). Your response to "the future is …" highlights your natural predisposition. At the same time, you must understand and consider your perspective does not necessarily match those around you—your family, friends, coworkers, and clients. Further, we often hold multiple beliefs about the future based on the particularities of the situation we find ourselves in. The future is a paradox.

Not just our attitude toward the future presents itself as a much more complex fractal, but also our ability to decode the future: the future is unwritten and inherently unknowable. As futurist and author Dr. Margaret Heffernan points out: "Anyone who tells you they can predict the future is probably just trying to own it" (2020). As we have seen with AT&T's PersonaLink video, particularly regarding technology, we can spot the emergent future if we look closely enough.

Want to know what the future of mobile phones would look like *before* Apple introduced the iPhone in 2007? Just look at General Magic's Magic Cap devices, which debuted in 1994; they had most of the features that made the iPhone such a success (though, of course, in a much cruder form). The handheld devices came with a touch-enabled graphical user interface sporting familiar, intuitive metaphors such as a desk complete with a mailbox, a Rolodex for your addresses, a notepad, and a little trash can. It even had a little digital cuckoo clock (yes, the weird Black Forest clocks with the wooden bird announcing the hour)—see also the next chapter. All of this worked nearly twenty years before the iPhone's debut—just slow and clunky, all the way down to how the device connected to the data network. Instead of using a sleek mobile wireless connection operating at megabits per second, you had to plug your telephone cable into a little port on the side of the device. General Magic was the future—just (much) too early.

The future truly is a paradox, encompassing seemingly contradictory positions: nonexistent but already here, unwritten but visible in signals all around us, a source of hope but also anxiety.

THE FUTURE IS UNCERTAIN

If the future is a paradox, how do we best embrace all its complexity and weirdness and make sense of it? In the early 1980s, software engineer Barry Boehm was the first to apply a concept from the world of engineering and construction in the chemical industry outside this niche sector: the Cone of Uncertainty (Boehm 1981). Charting the amount of uncertainty over the lifespan of a project, the cone of uncertainty provides a valuable tool to create better estimates and projections in areas ranging from complex engineering projects to hurricane forecasts. The further we look into the future, the deeper and greater the uncertainty we're stepping into becomes.

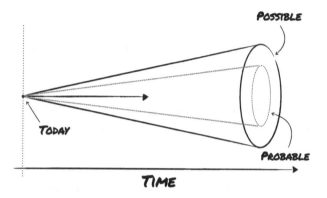

The Cone of Uncertainty

When we look at the future as an ever-expanding timeline—a future exists a day, a week, a month, a year, a decade from now—we assume a singular and linear future. A single line connects where we are today to the official future. But the future is uncertain. Instead of a neatly drawn line, our future is an expanding cone of probable futures (plural, not singular) surrounded by an even wider cone of possible futures. Our role as leaders in today's world of heightened uncertainty and complexity is to explore and decode those cones' upper and lower edges and then chart our course through these boundaries—creating an intentional and preferred future.

By welcoming uncertainty into our perspective on the future instead of engaging in a futile attempt to control it, uncertainty becomes a window into a world of possibilities.

Remember: you don't have *a* future. You have *many* futures.

THE FUTURE IS EXPONENTIAL

Nearly sixty years ago, Gordon Moore, cofounder of chip maker Intel, predicted the number of transistors on an integrated circuit would double every two years. Moore's prediction became known as "Moore's Law" and has held steady for six decades. His insight is why your mobile phone is (much) more powerful than a supercomputer from the 1980s and orders of magnitude more powerful than the computer which brought humans safely to the moon in 1969 (Intel n.d.).

Thirty years before Gordon Moore, Theodore Paul Wright—a US aeronautical engineer and educator—studied the vibrant airplane manufacturing industry. He observed the labor requirement was reduced by 10–15 percent for every doubling in airplane production. He later published his findings, today referred to simply as "Wright's Law" (Ark Invest 2020). In simple terms, Wright found in the world of technology, for every doubling in production, the cost drops by a fixed percentage: the more you make of something, the cheaper it gets, and progress becomes a flywheel. Wright's Law, as shown in a Santa Fe Institute paper (Nagy et al. 2012), applies to countless technological innovations, from the automobile to the television, modern battery technologies, and microchips (making Moore's Law merely a particular case of Wright's Law).

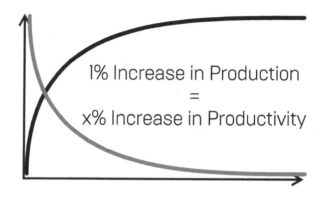

Wright's Law

The importance of Wright's Law in decoding the future cannot be underestimated: as we start producing more of a particular gadget and learn how to manufacture the gadget better, cheaper, and faster, the price falls. As the gadget becomes more affordable, we open up new, bigger markets, leading to more demand resulting in more units being manufactured, which in turn get cheaper and cheaper, leading to more and more demand. Once the flywheel starts, it keeps accelerating. (*) This is, of course, great for consumers: they get better products for less money as time goes by. A cheap Android smartphone today is much more capable and powerful than the same device at a much higher price only a few years ago.

For companies, this presents an interesting dilemma, though: follow the path of Wright's Law and maintain your revenue by selling more and more cheaper devices, or do what Apple does. By maintaining their technological edge, constantly pushing new advancements and features, all the while relentlessly focusing on their customers' needs, the iPhone remains at the top of the market, allowing the company to maintain their generous profit margins. Apple is surfing the crest of the smartphone wave.

(*) NB: This is true to a point: no development is exponential ad infinitum but flattens out over time, effectively creating an S-curve. Applying Wright's Law to this, demand eventually declines (the demand for a particular product or service is never unlimited), which leads to a smoothing out of the learning curve. Remember, the learning curve follows the demand curve. For our purposes, we focus on the first two-thirds of the resulting S-curve—what Geoffrey Moore calls the "incubation and transformation zone."

Plotting Wright's Law (and Moore's Law, for that matter) on a curve reveals the exponential nature of the effect—which also unveils the challenge we have with exponentials: our brains struggle to process them. What looks like very little change in the beginning suddenly turns steeply upwards. To quote Ernest Hemingway from his book *The Sun Also Rises* (1954), the future happens "gradually, then suddenly."

AT&T announced it would discontinue PersonaLink on July 11, 1996—nearly to the day, a year after Amazon started selling books on the internet (Howe 1996). Predicting how the future will play out is hard, for all the reasons outlined earlier. But hard doesn't mean impossible. All this raises the question: How do we know what comes next?

TL;DR

When making predictions about the future, consider the following points:

- Making definitive predictions about the future is impossible.
- Identifying early signs/indicators of possible futures is possible.
- Our beliefs and biases shape our view of the future.
- The further we project into the future, the greater the uncertainty and the wider the array of possible futures becomes.
- The future is increasingly being influenced by exponentially accelerating technologies.

1.2
Weak Signal
Detection

These waves of technology, you can see them way before they happen, and you just have to choose wisely which ones you're going to surf.

—STEVE JOBS

Did you know there's a game console that's also a pregnancy test? Six months into the COVID-19 lockdown, a computer hacker, who goes by the nickname Foone, decided to buy a digital pregnancy test. The pen-sized device can be purchased over the counter for about $3.50 and is a single-use, disposable device. Foone became curious about the device's inner workings and did what every good hacker does: they took it apart.

Once removed from its protective plastic casing, a standard pregnancy test revealed itself (the typical test strip which reacts to human chorionic gonadotropin, hCG). A sensor reading the results from the test transmits the data to a computer chip powered by a battery to show on a display if you are pregnant or not (Foone 2020).

Foone didn't stop here; they started researching the price and computational power of the chip being used on the device. Remember: this is a single-use, disposable test; most of us wouldn't consider it a "computer." Foone found something remarkable: the chip costs mere pennies yet has roughly the same computing power as the original IBM PC from 1981—the very device which gave the world Word and Excel and formed the launchpad for Bill Gates's Microsoft empire. All available today in an over-the-counter pregnancy test. And because Foone is a hacker, they put the computer game Doom on the pregnancy test so you can hunt demons on a Mars colony while waiting for your results. And no, it's not really a fully playable version of the genre-defining computer game—instead, a functioning, self-running demo. Still … it makes you wonder what it says about our view of humanity if we choose to entertain ourselves with the monster-slaying video game Doom while waiting for our pregnancy test results.

You might be laughing now or thinking "we have come a long, long way" since those early days of computing when an IBM PC cost $1,565 on its launch day some forty years ago (about $5,500 in today's money). I invite you to look at this as a weak signal, an early indicator of change, or as the historian, Fernand Braudel said, "a thin wisp of tomorrow" (1995). And don't just reflect on where we came from, but consider the far-reaching implications these developments can have for the future. Imagine the disruptive potential when you can deploy thousands of IBM PC-equivalent "computers" for a handful of dollars. We live in a moment which computer scientist Allen Wirfs-Brock describes as "ambient": computers are everywhere and just there; you don't even think about these devices as computers anymore.

It doesn't stop here. The world changed significantly every time we changed the scale of our computers, from room-filling mainframes to fridge-sized mini-computers to personal computers on our desks, laptops in our backpacks, and smartphones in our back pockets today. The companies dominating this world also changed: from IBM to Digital Equipment, Microsoft to Apple and Google—every time the scale changed, the companies dominating the market changed. These changes left mass casualties in their wake. All the companies that couldn't transition from one era to the next—UNIVAC, Data General, DEC, and countless others—have vanished. Others still, such as Microsoft, missed their chance to play in the new world; they no longer make mobile phones.

A digital pregnancy test becomes a weak signal—not just for diagnostic medical devices but for the world at large. The implications of this particular signal, where computers have become insanely cheap, radiate out to a world where disposable, abundant, ambient-type computation has become reality. And the consequences of this are vast: from smart manufacturing, where we put artificial intelligence into every machine on the shop floor, to lightbulbs automatically switching themselves off when you leave the house—tiny computers will be (and somewhat already are) ubiquitous.

SIGNALS ARE EVERYWHERE
AND EASY TO (DIS)MISS

Weak signals, the early harbingers of change, are everywhere—in our technologies, behaviors, and systems. They are easy to miss and dismiss. Consider Amara's Law: "We tend to overestimate the effect of a technology in the short run and underestimate the effect in the long run" (The VirtuLab n.d.). Weak signals often go unnoticed as they are typically crappy, expensive, and often not even properly working versions of a possible future existing at the fringes of business and society. Yet, learn to detect them, and the future can be unlocked.

In the late spring of 2013, I had the questionable honor of being one of the early testers for Google Glass—the heavily mocked augmented reality glasses Google's cofounder Sergey Brin touted as the future of computer interfaces. The day I received the email announcing my pair was ready for pickup, I walked across the Google campus to the Google X building—my springy step fueled by excitement about the new product propelling me forward. After receiving my Glass, I realized three things on my thirty-minute walk back to my office: firstly, Glass's functionality was mediocre at best. Secondly, the low battery warning light was already blinking. And thirdly—upon seeing myself in the mirror—I looked like an idiot wearing Google Glass.

A classic case of disappointment with the early iterations of a technology (the weak signals) and easy to dismiss. Yet, technology evolves, gets better and better, and eventually, we will wear genuinely "smart" glasses and gaze straight ahead instead of down when we want to use the power of our digital devices.

We are swimming in an ocean of weak signals; they truly are everywhere once you open your senses to them. By deliberately seeking diverse and different inputs, surrounding yourself with people who are *not* like you, and immersing yourself in their cultures, you will start detecting weak signals in abundance.

On a leisurely stroll around the NASA Ames campus during a warm Northern California summer's night with Guy Kawasaki, the legendary technology evangelist revealed his secret to me. In the early 1980s, Kawasaki breathed life into the Apple Macintosh together with his former boss Steve Jobs. Since then, he has been a highly successful "signal spotter." Chuckling over my admiration-filled question of how on earth he was able to successfully spot signal after signal (and thus predict many trends and shifts in the industry, such as streaming music services and online marketplaces for graphic design resources), he pointed out humans are sense-seeking and sense-making machines: "Our brain constantly filters out observations which don't fit the pattern; our survival autopilot is superb at filtering signal from noise." Leaning over, his voice conspicuously lowered, Kawasaki continued, "The problem with this behavior is you miss the weak signals as, by definition, they don't fit into your existing patterns." He paused, looked over his shoulder to check that nobody was listening, and revealed his secret. "Instead of looking away when you see something which doesn't fit into your pattern—something weird, strange, different—pause and ask yourself: 'Isn't that interesting?'"

The seemingly innocent question, when applied regularly, stops you in your tracks, overrides your signal/noise filter, and allows you to stay in discovery mode. Next time you come across something which feels, looks, or sounds out of the ordinary, or maybe even outright strange—a piece of odd technology, a teenager using their technology in an unusual way, or someone talking about a development you haven't heard of before—pause for a second, channel your inner Guy Kawasaki, and ask: Isn't that interesting?

Ever since that delightful evening in Mountain View, California, I ask myself this very question at least once a day, record the signal I spotted in a little journal, and frequently revisit it to detect any changes.

Isn't that interesting?

FROM NOISE TO SIGNAL

"Any sufficiently advanced technology is indistinguishable from magic." The famous quote by science fiction writer Arthur C. Clarke (2013) proved to be true in the early 1990s when, as a computer-obsessed teenager, I stumbled upon a *Macworld* magazine article describing a seemingly magical device. The little black unit was developed by a small, red-hot company founded by some of the same people who built the Apple Macintosh (and changed the way we think about computers forever): General Magic. Magic Cap, the operating system developed by General Magic, running on small, portable, network-connected handheld devices, provided an early glimpse into the future of mobile computing—a tantalizing yet woefully inadequate picture of a world where we have the world's information at our fingertips, anytime, anywhere. The article made me go "Woah!"; a vivid picture of the future presented itself to me on those pages. Alas, this future was inaccessible, expensive, and of limited use.

I took notice, clipped the article (those were the days of us reading magazines still printed on glossy paper), and kept revisiting the space. A weak signal was emerging from the ocean of press releases, commentary, and data points.

A few years later, while working for the most prominent German Apple retailer to spiff up my meager existence as a student, US Robotics' PalmPilot was released: a (relatively) cheap handheld device with a touch-sensitive screen and multiple built-in apps to manage your digital life, packaged into a form factor that made carrying the device everywhere a breeze. Looking at a PalmPilot today, one can easily see its resemblance with the iPhone or any Android phone; it was not only the spiritual predecessor but the direct ancestor of the generation-defining device unleashed on the world by Apple's founder Steve Jobs in 2007. With the release of the PalmPilot in 1997, the weak signal which we first spotted with the General Magic announcement started to take shape and grow.

A year after the PalmPilot launched, I helped a friend start a software company for PalmPilot apps. It was crude (you installed apps by connecting your PalmPilot with a serial cable, using special software to transfer an "app" from a floppy disk you bought from a store or mail order company); yet, it was a clear precursor of the times to be. The weak signal emerged from the noise and presented a clear, compelling vision of the future: small, connected computers in everybody's pocket, running apps informing and entertaining us.

Curiosity allowed us to see the early glimpses of a future long before it materialized. Continuous reexamination of the space provided the insight to sort signals from noise. And a little game of "What if?" combined with "How might we?" presented young me with the opportunity to be early in an emerging market and be part of a company that rode the breaking wave of an unfolding future. My friend's company became a dominant player in the burgeoning market for PalmPilot software. My involvement in his company laid the groundwork for my early career in computers and mobile devices—including a short-lived but highly entertaining (and lucrative) episode of me importing the first iPhone from the US into Germany.

Yet, after purchasing my first PalmPilot, I had to wait ten years for the true vision of the iPhone to become a reality.

NB: It is worth pointing out that we focus on specific types of signals in the context of this book—those leading to improved or new products, services, or business solutions. The intrepid reader, curious about the larger scope of signals, such as social and societal signals, may want to dig deeper into the canon of the forecasting literature.

TL;DR

To hone your weak signal detection capabilities, consider the following points:

- Stay "switched on" as a continuous, reflexive behavior and pay attention to marginal practices, peculiar behaviors, and odd appropriation/repurposing of technologies.
- Catalog your findings and look for connections between technologies, use cases, and behaviors.
- Revisit the stimuli regularly—at least every six months—and explore what has changed.

1.3

Strong Signal Spotting

I'm only suggesting that we properly gauge the difficulty of whatever we are told could be the next big thing. If the idea builds on practical experience, then guarded optimism is in order. If not, then not. Hope is a scarce thing; we shouldn't squander it.
—RODNEY BROOKS, COMPUTER SCIENTIST AND IEEE FELLOW

Cue the CueCat. At the turn of the millennium, Jeffry Jovan Philyaw unveiled a cat-shaped handheld barcode reader that was given away for free to millions of internet users. In case you don't remember the CueCat, here is the Museum of Failure describing the device and its functionality (not that the source of this definition might be an indicator of where the story is going):

Marketed as a revolutionary technology, the CueCat, a cat-shaped handheld scanner, plugged into your computer. By scanning special codes in printed magazines, users could open the advertisers' websites without entering the web address. Millions were produced and shipped free with magazines such as *Wired* and *Businessweek*. The device was pitched as a way to avoid typing in long web addresses [...] (Museum of Failure 2022).

Despite millions of the cat-shaped devices being produced and shipped across the USA to subscribers of those magazines, somehow someone forgot to ask how reading your magazine of choice in front of your computer to scan the little barcodes on ads is better than simply typing an internet address. The device failed spectacularly. By the end of 2001, the CueCat stopped working, and in the process, Philyaw changed his legal name to Jovan Hutton Pulitzer—an outcome which, in hindsight, seems obvious and unavoidable (apart from Philyaw changing his name; that feels drastic by most standards). Yet, when the CueCat came out, it did so to the deafening fanfare of an overly excited press hailing the device as the future of media consumption. A few short years later, the same press outlets called it "the #1 worst invention of the decade" (Barrett 2009). Technology journalist Walt Mossberg lamented in the *Wall Street Journal* (2000) "to scan in codes from magazines and newspapers, you have to be reading them in front of your PC. That's unnatural and ridiculous."

The little device, resembling a cat ready to pounce, was a weak signal—one which, like so many others, fizzled out instead of making it big with a loud bang heard across the business press.

By far, not every weak signal will turn into a strong one. Strong signals are the ones successfully moving from hype to reality, the ones shifting from potential to actual disruption—the iPhone and not the CueCat. This begets the million-dollar questions: "What makes a weak signal tip?" and "When will a weak signal turn into a strong one?"

NB: Decades and a global pandemic later, we now have rather ubiquitous QR codes, delivering much of the same functionality as the CueCat. However, to scan a QR code, you use a device always with you, highly mobile, and incredibly powerful—your smartphone. And it took COVID-19 and the move away from paper menus in restaurants for hygiene reasons to make QR codes widely used and accepted.

ANATOMY OF A SIGNAL

Weak signals take time to mature—usually, much longer than we might think. In 2008 *Fortune* magazine's senior editor Betsy Morris talked to Steve Jobs about his uncanny ability to decode weak signals and spot not only those turning into blockbuster hits, but also predict with high accuracy the right time to launch a new product leveraging the decoded signal. Jobs remarked candidly:

Things happen fairly slowly, you know. They do. These waves of technology, you can see them way before they happen, and you just have to choose wisely which ones you're going to surf. If you choose unwisely, then you can waste a lot of energy, but if you choose wisely, it actually unfolds fairly slowly. It takes years (Elmer-Dewitt 2008).

This gives us our first clue—technology moves fast, but not nearly as quickly as it appears from afar. Hemingway's insight that things happen "gradually, then suddenly" is a good one to remember in this context.

The challenge is that once a signal reaches the tipping point, markets (and market leaders) are regularly made within a feverishly short six to eighteen months. In a hyper-connected, globalized world, companies have little time to react, to move into pole position, and to be ready when the conditions for a weak signal to become a strong one become just right. Those who cross the race's finish line first enjoy a five-to-seven-year period of exponential growth and margins, as Geoffrey Moore showed in his seminal book *Zone to Win* (2015).

To reference a somewhat overused yet poignant example: the iPhone took the world by storm and, shortly after its release in 2007, dominated not only smartphone but mobile phone sales. Apple has kept its market-leader position ever since—and harvested massive profits. The same happened with Apple's tablet computer, the iPad, and its smartwatch, the Apple Watch. The company has an eerie ability to get its timing right and launch its products in maturing categories at the perfect moment to make the market, take the leadership position, and remain there for years. As Apple shows us, you don't need (and often don't want) to be first to market in order to dominate an industry.

In our research, and by cross-referencing the tools and frameworks of the world's best trend researchers, we identified three filters allowing you to sift through weak signals. The filters determine a weak signal's potential to turn into a strong signal and allow you to make predictions of the moment a gradual change will turn into a sudden one.

Technology moves fast. But how fast is "fast" really?

MATURITY

Hype or reality? What separates the two is often the maturity of the underlying technology. When evaluating the moment a weak signal ripened enough to tip over into a strong signal (and thus shift from hype to reality) we rate the maturity of a signal on a scale from zero to ten. This applies especially when it comes to technology.

Maturity Scale

On our scale, zero is a physically impossible technology. Before you shake your head and ask why one would even consider this point on the scale, remind yourself of the spectacularly failed medical testing company Theranos. Using a single drop of blood, Theranos promised to provide an array of precise blood tests and biomarkers. After a $700 million investment, the market woke up to the fact the technology

Theranos promised was physically impossible—a zero on our maturity scale.

When moving from the realm of the impossible to the space where things are possible, they become scientific problems to solve, from the theoretically possible (a one on our scale) to the experimental/lab phase. As the signal matures, it slowly but surely moves from the lab into production, becoming an engineering challenge (somewhere around the midway point on our scale). Lastly, once the signal has further matured, and with it our ability to scale it to a mass market, the engineering challenge turns into a business one.

Using serial entrepreneur Elon Musk and his many ventures as examples, we can see how the scale applies. Musk's successful companies are all operating well inside the "business challenge" range: from electric vehicle maker Tesla to solar panel installer SolarCity, internet satellite company Starlink, and the tunnel drilling operations at The Boring Company. These companies are built on mature, well-understood, and scalable technologies (even when Musk infamously broke the "unbreakable" windscreen on the Tesla Cybertruck during its launch event). Rocket company SpaceX started in the realm of engineering challenges: the specific fin design, which allows Musk's rockets to land and thus be reused, was invented by Russian scientists in the 1970s but couldn't be scaled for commercial use until recently. And Musk's vision for hyper-speed rail transport, Hyperloop, still has many unanswered scientific questions to sort out (chief among them: How do we safely accelerate and decelerate the "train" without injuring the passengers in the required short amount of time?).

Assessing a weak signal on the timing scale gives you a good sense of where the signal is today and what is necessary for the signal to turn from a weak one into a strong one. As Rodney Brooks in our opening quote reminds us, "If the idea builds on practical experience, then guarded optimism is in order. If not, then not" (2018).

Unless you deliberately want to push technology development forward or play a highly speculative game, don't invest your time and energy into any signal that isn't at least a solid seven on the maturity scale.

GESTALT

This unique word conceptually only exists in German, *gestalt* being a collection of physical, biological, psychological, or symbolic entities creating a unified concept, configuration, or pattern greater than the sum of its parts.

We use the word to describe the surrounding factors of a weak signal, which either provide a head- or tailwind to the speed with which a signal matures. In other words: What dependencies do you have little to no control over which either speed up or slow down the development and adoption of the signal in question?

Often overlooked, these factors can be instrumental in accelerating or decelerating the speed with which signals move and sometimes provide even a complete roadblock to a weak signal. To assess the gestalt of a weak signal, apply the acronym STEEPS: What are the scientific (S), technological (T), environmental (E), economic (E), political (P), and social (S) factors which either need to be in place or need to be removed for a signal to progress from weak to strong?

Reed Hastings, streaming media giant Netflix's founder and CEO, has many factors he and his team can directly influence: setting up server farms for their streaming media content, writing software, and creating their own content. But Netflix has little to no control over at least one factor which is paramount to their success: the proliferation of broadband internet. If you still use a dial-up internet connection, you will not stream the latest Hollywood blockbuster to your television.

Returning to the spiritual successor of the CueCat, QR codes, their recent rise to ubiquity was fueled by a fear of COVID-19—a fear which shifted the gestalt in favor of the little dotted square.

Mapping out the gestalt of a weak signal is an often overlooked yet vital step to increase our ability to predict the future of a signal with high(er) certainty.

UTILITY

Lastly, never forget to consider the actual utility (or usefulness) of the signal at hand. Chris Yeh, the coauthor of the *New York Times* bestselling book *Blitzscaling*, uses three lenses to assess a product's or service's utility: What are the problem's frequency, density, and friction the proposed solution aims to solve? (Hoffman and Yeh 2018).

By answering three simple questions, you can quickly and accurately assess if a proposed solution has enough utility to make the leap from weak to strong signal:

- How often do you encounter the problem the product or service aims to solve? (Frequency)
- How much time and energy do you spend in the problem space when you encounter the problem? (Density)
- How much pain does the problem cause you? (Friction)

Going back to our feline friend, the CueCat: the problem the CueCat devices aimed to solve was for users to not have to type URLs from print advertisements into their internet browser. Considering the three factors, we realize quickly the frequency of us typing in a URL from a print ad is low, the time and energy (and thus density) it requires doing so is relatively minimal, and the pain of this is negligible (friction). The CueCat was a solution to a problem that didn't exist.

Signal spotting, using the three filters above, allows us, if applied carefully, to make grounded predictions about the potential of a weak signal turning strong, as well as the moment in time this will happen. You will escape the blinding flashlights of the ever-present hype machine and make a realistic prediction of the impact and timing of disruptive innovations.

Which begets the question: What even is disruption?

TL;DR

To separate weak from strong signals, consider the following points:

- Evaluate frankly the maturity of the individual technologies making up the signal. Often, a signal is the combination of underlying technologies (e.g., the Metaverse consists of headset technologies, connectivity, servers, tooling, etc.).
- Assess all the dependencies (gestalt) that provide head- or tailwinds in developing and adopting the signal.
- Determine the mid- to long-term utility of the signal; a good litmus test is the question, "Can you imagine a world where *this* will not be true?"

PART TWO:
DISRUPT

2
Disrupting the Future

I have seen the future, and it works.

—LINCOLN STEFFENS

"I'm a terrified dinosaur." Jorge Paulo Lemann—cofounder of 3G Capital, the multibillion-dollar investment firm which owns, among many other things, a majority stake in the world's largest beer brewer, AB InBev—confessed this in early 2018 at the Milken Institute Global Conference. Lemann continued:

I've been living in this cozy world of old brands, big volumes. Nothing changes very much, and you could just focus on being very efficient, and you'd be okay. And all of a sudden, we are being disrupted in all ways (Gara 2018).

He is right. We truly live in extraordinary, exponential, and disruptive times, times that can be summarized in a simple sentence: tomorrow will look dramatically different than today.

Combustion engine cars are increasingly replaced by electric vehicles and cable TV is being upended by streaming video services. Travel agencies are being made obsolete by booking sites on the internet. The COVID-19 pandemic brought widespread disruptions with it. You'd be hard pressed to name an industry or sector which is not going through turbulent times and in the process will dramatically shift the way it looks, feels, and operates. Disruption makes old things obsolete (in contrast to its close cousin, "innovation," which is all about doing the same things, just better).

Disruption is the new normal—and incredibly hard to do right. Management guru Clayton Christensen found 95 percent of new product innovations fail (MIT 2022), and the Startup Genome Project showed 92 percent of all startups share the same fate (2022). Meanwhile, consulting firm Innosight predicts 50 percent of Fortune 500 companies will be replaced within the next ten years (Mochari 2016). And you can't open the newspaper, read a business magazine, or browse the internet without seeing, reading, or hearing the word "disruption." Google Trends registered a more than 60 percent increase in search volume for the term in the fifteen years from 2004 to 2019—before COVID-19 further ramped these numbers up to stratospheric heights (2022).

Using the sophisticated analytics tools of his company Sprinklr, Marshall Kirkpatrick determined that on Wednesday, July 21, 2021—a typical summer's day—the word "disruption" was mentioned a staggering 18,000 times on the internet. Interestingly, the term was used primarily by news websites and management consultancies—but very little on Twitter (the preeminent social media hub), nor by futurists.

It appears the futurists have absorbed the term into their day-to-day, whereas the word still rings true in the land of the consultants.

The term is used in myriad ways, typically without clear definition or delineation from its cousins, innovation and transformation. A quick Google search brings up "disruption warfare" or "Disruption Bambi," with the first suggestion being "disruption synonym"—not "meaning" or "definition," but "synonym"—which already tells you something about our understanding of the term. You might be as confused about "Disruption Bambi" as I was: Disruption Bambi is a character in the online game Bambi Land; hilariously, it is the primary opponent to a character called "Disruption."

The earliest definition for the word "disruption" dates back more than 500 years and defines disruption as a "breaking apart, a rending asunder, a forcible separation into parts." (Online Etymology Dictionary 2022) Having its origin in the Latin word *disruptio,* the term originated in the field of medicine (referring to a "laceration of tissue"), which only much later made its way into the broader vocabulary. Today's use of the word disruption as a "radical change to an existing industry or market due to technological innovation" didn't appear until Clayton Christensen coined the term "disruptive innovation" in his seminal 1997 bestselling book, *The Innovator's Dilemma* (2015).

Since the release of Christensen's bestseller, we have seen an explosion of the term and its usage. Online book review site Goodreads lists 3,454 books with the word disruption in their title (2022)—not counting the book you are currently reading. And this doesn't include all the books writing about disruption without putting the word directly into the title. Google has indexed well above a billion pages for the search term "disruption" (2022). And podcast search engine Listen Notes returns more than 10,000 episodes talking about the topic (2022).

Let's put this out there: disruption has become tofu. Yes, tofu, the curd made from mashed soybeans, chiefly used in Asian and vegetarian cooking. The stuff tastes like nothing until you put sauce on it—which makes it taste like the sauce. Disruption is the same: it has lost its original meaning, is being used haphazardly, and takes on the flavor of its surrounding context.

Yet, fundamentally understanding the inner workings of disruptive change is paramount for any leader of any business in any industry. Once understood, navigating these turbulent times becomes a much easier undertaking—and one with a much higher chance of success. You certainly don't want to find yourself at a large, important conference, openly admitting to having become a dinosaur.

It is time to decode and disrupt disruption.

2.1

Disrupt Disruption

You promised me Mars colonies. Instead, I got Facebook.

—*BUZZ ALDRIN*

Kodak, Blockbuster, and Nokia. When we talk about disruption, a set of stories are repeated ad nauseam; this trifecta describes the rise and rapid decline of these former industry titans. All were pioneers and dominant market leaders in their respective fields, so much so they were synonymous with their respective industries. And all of them were disrupted and went under within a few short years. Yet, much can (still) be learned from the once mighty colossuses.

THE DISRUPTION TRIFECTA

Kodak's employee Steven Sasson invented the digital camera in 1975. Sasson went on to fight a long and ultimately fruitless challenge to convince Kodak's leadership team the future was, indeed, digital (Estrin 2015). The company lost the first battle to create cheap digital cameras, which flooded the market and encouraged their owners to take photos—lots of photos—but not necessarily have them immortalized on paper. Remember, Kodak made most of its money by selling film and, more importantly, developing prints. The second blow came when phones and cameras merged, and suddenly, we all were equipped with not only a camera but also the perfect viewing device for the many, many pictures we took (rendering the need to develop photos obsolete). The final blow came the moment when Marc Andreessen famously pointed out "software ate the world" (2011). All our digital memories became easily accessible, searchable, and backed up by smartphone apps and cloud storage.

Pundits love to make fun of Blockbuster, the company which dominated home video entertainment like no other. Blockbuster launched a formidable DVD mail-order rental business, which it shut down shortly after as it couldn't see how the business would ever make any money and not cannibalize its existing stores. Ironically, it also had multiple opportunities to acquire upstart Netflix at highly favorable terms. A few short years after it dismissed the threat of Netflix, Blockbuster shuttered store after store—until a sole store, located in a Central Oregon strip mall 170 miles east of Portland, remained. In a cruel twist of history, the store and its owners became the stars of a Netflix documentary fittingly called *The Last Blockbuster* (Associated Press 2021). To add insult to injury, Netflix recently produced a sitcom about life in a Blockbuster store. A truly cautionary tale of "what could have been"—and one which we will dissect in more detail soon.

And, of course, Nokia—the legendary purveyor of the finest, most sought-after mobile phones. In November 2007, *Forbes* boldly headlined its namesake magazine with the rhetorical question, "Nokia—One Billion Customers. Can Anyone Catch the Cell Phone King?" (2007). The fortunes of Nokia changed dramatically within a few short years after Steve Jobs showed thousands of visitors in the packed Moscone Convention Center in San Francisco "one more thing." Jobs jokingly presented an iPod with a rotary phone dial mounted on it, quipping Apple finally created the iPhone, before going on and fishing the revolutionary device out of his pocket. Around the same time, not far from Apple's headquarters in Cupertino (California), Google introduced the Android smartphone operating system to the world—which slowly but surely became the dominant mobile phone operating system globally.

Meanwhile, Nokia's mobile phone business went from an overpriced and ill-advised acquisition by Microsoft to a fire sale to the Finish company HMD Global. Nokia today is merely a brand slapped onto Android-based phones—a weak shadow of its former self. Years after Nokia's fall from grace, Nokia's former CEO Stephen Elop still couldn't admit defeat and defended himself by saying, "We didn't do anything wrong, but somehow, we lost" (Top Video Corner 2016). I am sure we can all think of dozens of things Nokia did indeed do wrong. Take for example Elop's infamous appearance on the Finnish television show *Hjalliksen kanssa*: when asked about Apple's foray into phones, Elop grabbed the iPhone from host Hjallis Harkimo, threw it onto the floor, and proclaimed, "There, it's gone" (MSPoweruser Power 2012). As the German proverb goes, *Der Fisch stinkt vom Kopf*—"the fish rots from the head down."

Everyone loves to regurgitate these stories—often to make their respective points about disruption happening faster than ever before and the fallacy of incumbents not being able to think about the future and act accordingly, or simply for a good chuckle. Laughing about someone else's mistake and, at least for a moment, not thinking about our own challenges are always nice.

If you are anything like me, you feel a little sick every time you hear these tales. The stories are too well-trodden and repetitive: the incumbent has everything going for them, typically even invents the future, but can't get out of their own way. We forget these companies seemed to be on top of their game, were staffed with talented leaders, and, for the most part, could see the disruption in their industry coming.

In effect, we not only grossly oversimplify a complex operational environment but look at only one side of the story. The question we ask is: "What can we learn from Apple, Netflix, or Instagram (i.e., the disruptors)?"

Of course, much can be learned from Steve Jobs at Apple, Reid Hastings at Netflix, or Kevin Systrom at Instagram (and many books have been written about these stories and their lessons learned). But we are missing a large and tremendously important part of the story when we don't look at the other side of disruption—the part of the story which looks not at the things that changed but the things that stayed the same.

JOBS TO BE DONE

In his book *Competing Against Luck*, Clayton Christensen laid out the concept of the jobs-to-be-done principle: "People don't simply buy products or services, they 'hire' them to make progress in specific circumstances" (2016).

Looking closer at our classic disruption stories, whether Kodak, Blockbuster, Nokia, or many others, we realize the underlying jobs to be done—the things we hired the product or service to do for us—haven't actually changed as the company in question got disrupted.

You still take photos—as a matter of fact, many, many more than ever before. They just don't happen to be on film anymore. At the peak of Kodak's rule over photographic film in 2000, the company sold a billion rolls of film—resulting in about 12 billion photos taken in the USA that year (Andrews 2022). Twenty years on, in 2020, humanity took a staggering 1.4 trillion photos—nearly exclusively digitally and on their mobile phones (Carrington 2022).

Likewise, you are still watching movies at home. Thankfully, they don't come in the form of VHS cassettes with their lousy image quality and the annoying necessity to rewind the tape before returning them, but in the form of streaming video delivered straight to our TVs—with Netflix being a market leader (T4 2021). And you almost certainly are watching more movies than during the days of Blockbuster's VHS cassettes.

You still hold a small device in your hand (and to your face) to stay in touch with the world wherever and whenever you want. But the specific way you do this has changed. Zoom has replaced the phone call, and WhatsApp has done the same for SMS; therefore, these are the companies dominating this industry.

The critical and often overlooked insight here is the underlying consumer needs—creating lasting mementos of our experiences, entertaining ourselves in the comfort of our homes, and staying in touch with our friends—don't change all that much over long periods. Our needs and wants tend to be incredibly durable. How durable, you might ask? Don't just look at recent disruptions but take the ones which have been with us for long periods—transportation, for example. Since the days of humans riding horses and buggies, going back to ancient Mesopotamia thousands of years ago, all the way to the latest fully autonomous, electricity-powered robot-taxi from the likes of Waymo, our underlying need (in Christensen's verbiage: our job-to-be-done) stayed consistent and the same: move from A to B in the least amount of time with the highest degrees of comfort and the lowest cost.

The takeaway is simple yet often overlooked: in the vast majority of "disruptions," the underlying job-to-be-done has never changed. Amazon's founder Jeff Bezos reiterated this point when asked about Amazon's big-picture strategy:

I very frequently get the question: "What's going to change in the next ten years?" And that is a very interesting question; it's a very common one. I almost never get the question: "What's not going to change in the next ten years?" And I submit to you the second question is actually the more important of the two—because you can build a business strategy around the things that are stable in time … . In our retail business, we know customers want low prices, and I know that's going to be true ten years from now. They want fast delivery; they want a vast selection. It's impossible to imagine a future ten years from now where a customer comes up and says, "Jeff, I love Amazon; I just wish the prices were a little higher," [or] "I love Amazon; I just wish you'd deliver a little more slowly." Impossible .... When you have something you know is true, even over the long term, you can afford to put a lot of energy into it (Amazon Web Services 2012).

Which begets an important question: If the need we hired the product or service to fulfill hasn't changed—what is disruption?

TL;DR
To gain a holistic view of disruption, consider the following points:

- Identify the job-to-be-done for your product or service. Remember, your customers don't buy your product or service; they hire them to make progress in specific circumstances.
- Consider not only what will be different but also what will *not* change as you think about the future.

2.2

The State Change Model

Nothing is so painful to the human mind as a great and sudden change.

—MARY WOLLSTONECRAFT SHELLEY,

FRANKENSTEIN

If how we do things changes (sometimes dramatically), but our customer needs and the underlying reasons don't—what could be a better way for us to talk and think about disruption? The world of physics offers a fitting analog: state changes.

Changes of state are physical changes in a matter. They are reversible changes and do not involve any changes in the chemical makeup of the matter. Common state changes include melting, freezing, sublimation, deposition, condensation, and vaporization (Byju's 2022).

Water is a simple example of why the concept maps so beautifully to the world of disruption. Put a pot of water in your freezer. After a little while, once it reaches zero degrees Celsius, the water turns into ice, a solid matter. Take the pot out of the freezer and wait long enough, and the ice returns to its liquid state. Now place the pot on your stove, and at 100 degrees Celsius it will start to boil and eventually transform one more time from its liquid state to vapor and thus a gaseous state. The shift from one form to the other is called a "state change."

The vital insight—and the reason we evoke this analogous model to talk about disruption—is the underlying molecule, H_2O, hasn't changed throughout this whole process. Whether you are holding a chunk of ice in your hand, sipping from a glass of water, or observing steam rising from a boiling pot, it is all H_2O. Now replace H_2O with your customers' jobs to be done, and you realize you have changed how we fulfill our customers' needs (the state), yet the need remains fundamentally the same (the job our product or service is hired to satisfy).

Remember the last time you cooked spaghetti? Standing in front of a big pot of water, cooker cranked up to the max, dry pasta in hand, you anxiously wait for the water to boil. Staring down at your big pasta pot, you see the first bubbles forming; experience (and the recipe) calls for the water to boil thoroughly before putting in the pasta. Time drags on; seemingly, it takes forever until the well-salted liquid reaches the right state. And when you turn around, bored with waiting, the water inevitably boils over with a loud hiss—story of my life.

Similar to state changes in the world of physics (and cooking), the transition from state to state in technology usually does not follow a linear progression but rather an exponential curve: state changes happen gradually, then suddenly.

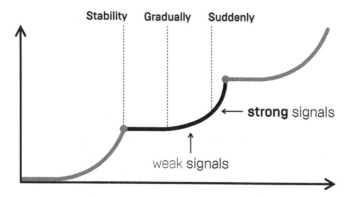

State Changes

The very same is happening in the world of business and technology. In the early stages of every state, you have stability; the world Jorge Paulo Lemann described as one where "you could just focus on being efficient, and you'd be okay" (Samor 2018). This initial phase of stability is where incumbents build a formidable moat around their castle. As long as you are good at what you do and are effective, efficient, and optimized, you have little to fear and much to gain. Size matters in this phase, and newcomers have a nearly insurmountable wall to climb should they try to break into your market.

But as with most good things in life, particular states never last forever. Eventually, you will see the early signs of change emerging. If you look carefully, you can see the weak signals materializing. Easily dismissed as anomalies, absurdities, and oddities on the fringes, they frequently go unnoticed until they gain momentum and gradually turn into strong(er) ones, which turn into full-blown sudden transitions from one state into the next. Once a state change is underway, the deepest moats, tallest walls, and strongest castles fall. This is why weak signal detection and strong signal spotting are essential skills to hone.

We used to make phone calls on landline phones in our homes and offices and used a telephone booth when we were out and about, until the overpriced and underpowered monstrosity of the first mobile phones became small and cheap enough to turn into a mass phenomenon. A state change had happened. Mobile phones lived through their own phase of stability, in the process turning Nokia into one of the most respected technology companies on the planet, until the crappy, hugely overpriced, underpowered, and plain awkward smartphones from the nineties evolved into a global sensation. It took the underlying technologies to mature enough for Steve Jobs and his team at Apple to package them into what Jobs hailed as "a phone, an iPod, a camera" (and so much more) to complete the next state change (Schroter 2011).

The same story can be told about essentially any other disruption: things are done one way until they aren't. Gradually, and then suddenly, states change, and with them, not just the way things are being done but often the companies dominating a particular state.

And make no mistake: state changes have been with us since time immemorial; they just happened much, much slower than they do today. Futurist Ray Kurzweil pointed out in his essay "The Law of Accelerating Returns" (2001) the rate of change itself is accelerating, resulting in humans not experiencing 100 years of progress in the twenty-first century but rather 20,000 years of progress at today's rate. We'd better get ready to live in a world of constant state changes—yet one where the underlying consumer needs, the jobs to be done, remain stable.

THE PERILS OF STATE CHANGES

State changes are tricky to navigate. When markets and organizations move from one state to the next, the underlying ways of doing things fundamentally change, which creates a whole array of problems for the incumbent.

Let's explore this through the example of Blockbuster—and no, we are not talking about Blockbuster to make fun of them or regurgitate one of the classics in the canon of disruption. Rather, we use Blockbuster as an easy-to-follow and perfect example of the perils of state changes.

In 1985, the year the Dire Straits topped the charts with their seminal hit "Money for Nothing," Tears for Fears proclaimed "Everybody Wants to Rule the World," and USA for Africa reminded us that "We Are the World," Blockbuster opened its first store in Dallas, Texas with 8,000 VHS tapes covering 6,500 titles—a massive collection compared to the typical mom-and-pop video rental stores which could be found in many cities around the US.

The company, founded by software entrepreneur David Cook, realized the highly fragmented and incredibly labor-intense market, where videotapes were kept behind the counter and had to be manually checked out by the store clerk, was ripe for automation and scale. Cook's inaugural store displayed tapes openly on bookshelves. Customers picked the movie they liked, walked to the counter, videotape in hand, and were checked out by using a computerized system leveraging laser scanners and barcodes printed on the back of the VHS cassette. Theft was prevented by small magnetic strips on the videos, which interacted with the security system in the door. The store was an immediate hit.

By the end of 1987, Blockbuster operated 133 stores. A series of acquisitions, combined with an aggressive growth strategy, saw Blockbuster grow to 700 stores within two years, and by the beginning of 1993, the iconic blue-and-yellow logo could be found on more than 3,400 stores worldwide. Blockbuster grew into adjacent areas such as video game and music rentals and merged with media giant Viacom for an eye-watering $4.7 billion. By the turn of the millennium, you could find a Blockbuster store within a ten-minute drive of virtually every major neighborhood in the United States (Company-Histories.com 2022). At its peak in 2004, Blockbuster counted 9,094 stores and employed approximately 84,300 people—58,500 in the United States and 25,800 in other countries (Zippia n.d.).

And this was the company's downfall: at its core, Blockbuster wasn't a company built to provide convenient home entertainment to its clients but a highly efficient, effective, and supremely optimized video rental business with strong expertise in real estate and store operations. Blockbuster's team knew better than any of their competitors which ZIP code to place a new store in and how to merchandise and run it. The company's core skills were singularly focused on being the world's best video rental store company—and they excelled at it. Blockbuster dominated the era of its market state—the VHS video rental market.

But states change. Some of these state changes take a while to manifest, but eventually and inevitably, they will happen. The VHS video cassette, a technology already nine years old even when Blockbuster was founded, was superseded by the much more capable and easier-to-handle DVD. Released in 1996, DVDs are vastly superior to VHS cassettes—in terms of video and audio quality, durability, and convenience. DVDs don't need to be rewound (a constant source of frustration for Blockbuster and its customers, leading to the slogan "Be Kind, Rewind"). And, as Reed Hastings, cofounder of Netflix, quickly realized, they can be put into an envelope and shipped cheaply.

Founded in 1997, long before Blockbuster eventually peaked in its expansion, the Netflix team realized they could solve multiple customer frustrations in the home video rental market simultaneously. Even if your next Blockbuster is only ten minutes away, driving to a store is tedious. Not getting the movie you'd like to watch, as the one you wanted to see was already rented out in your local store, and paying high fees for returning the tape a day late were all annoyances Netflix solved with their mail order-inspired rental model. Add to this Netflix's automated recommendation system, introduced in 2000, and the state for home video rental shifted dramatically.

State changes present a grave danger for incumbents. As a company adapts from one state to the next, its existing skills and processes become irrelevant. Blockbuster's investments in its in-store movie rental business (in terms of people, process, and capital expenditure) became obsolete the moment DVD mail order rental became a reality. It doesn't matter that Blockbuster was the world's best video rental store real estate company. Once the state shifted from VHS tapes in a store to DVDs via mail order, what mattered was the ability to run a highly efficient, effective, and supremely optimized mail order company. You don't need to know which ZIP codes your stores ought to be in, how closely located each store must be from the next, or how to run the most efficient checkout process. In the new state, you need to figure out how to integrate your warehouses deeply with your shipping partners and how to run highly optimized pick/pack/ ship operations.

For incumbents whose existing skills and processes have become obsolete, a dual challenge presents itself: firstly, you must build supreme skills and processes to operate in the new state (and build associated investments into infrastructure). Secondly, you need to figure out how to move your old operations that are quickly becoming obsolete (including both capital and operational expenditure) into the new state (or shed them altogether). All this becomes a challenge compounded by an often-necessary shift in operations and culture. New states require companies to act and think fundamentally differently about how they fulfill their customers' needs and wants. Add to this the occurring shifts in economic models which go hand in hand with state changes, and the result is the most complex challenge in any business at any time. Consider, for example, the transition from paying per rented videotape to a watch-as-much-as-you-want rental fee, as was the case with Netflix.

And, of course, the states keep changing. From DVDs, we went to streaming video. Instead of running a mail order business with all its operational aspects, the challenge becomes running a technology business: from managing server farms, writing user-facing software like mobile apps, negotiating placements on streaming media devices, to working with content producers to secure streaming media rights—the necessary skills and processes to be successful in a world of streaming media are markedly different from those required to run a mail order DVD rental business or a VHS video rental store chain.

We now know, of course, Reed Hastings's team at Netflix managed this transition from one state to the next near flawlessly—mainly because Hastings knew the DVD was only a transitory state; streaming is a state with much more staying power. Therefore, Netflix could anticipate the state change and prepare itself and its people for the inevitable.

State changes create profoundly disruptive environments for incumbents to operate in. One can spot state changes everywhere by zooming out from the Blockbuster/Netflix example and applying the insights and lessons learned in other industries and markets. Take the transition of owning your (combustion engine-powered) car to a world where we subscribe to transportation services, à la Uber (using fleets of autonomous electric vehicles), as just one example.

As leaders, we must fundamentally understand our product or service's job for our clients (from their perspective), assess the current state in which we fulfill our clients' needs, and scan for potential changes to the state. Once a weak signal indicating a state change is spotted and assessed using the strong-signal-spotting filter from the earlier chapter on strong signal spotting, leaders can and must engage in preparing their organization for the upcoming shift.

Which leaves us with a critical question: How do you spot a state change?

TL;DR
To anticipate, prepare for, and leverage state changes, consider the following points:

- The way we do things (the state) changes, yet the underlying needs (the jobs to be done) are typically stable.
- You are currently operating in a specific state; each state is either in a phase of stability, experiencing gradual changes, or suddenly transitioning into a new state.
- The biggest challenge of a state change is the incumbent's misaligned expertise, experience, and processes—all of which are focused on the current state.

2.3

The Relevance of Sustainable Relevance

There is no fate but what we make for ourselves.

—JOHN CONNOR,
TERMINATOR 3: RISE OF THE MACHINES

Blockbuster's demise and Netflix's rise directly result from a particular state change—the shift from VHS to DVDs. Sure enough, the home entertainment industry is not the only industry that went, goes, and will go through state changes. Industry after industry, sector after sector, state changes are everywhere and constant. And herein lies the perils of state changes: they tend to sneak up on us (remember Hemingway's "gradually, then suddenly") and are easily dismissed in their early incarnations as "not good enough," "too expensive," or simply wacky and weird. But once they materialize, incumbents frequently trip over their hesitancy to act decisively and swiftly, overcome encrusted organizational structures, and shed engrained behaviors when trying to react to the new reality.

Andy Billings, head of creative profitability at computer game maker Electronic Arts (where his responsibility is to ensure business and creativity not only go hand in hand but accelerate each other), pointed out in a long conversation with me over a spotty Zoom connection at the beginning of the COVID-19 pandemic in mid-2020, "the game we are in is one of sustainable relevance. How do you ensure you keep catching the right wave and surf it well?"

Sustainable relevance—your ability to achieve and maintain product/market fit, of delivering a product or service which fulfills your customers' needs (their job-to-be-done) and does so across state changes—is key to your organization's long-term viability and success. Billings's company is a good example: fueling its customers' desire for play and entertainment, the company successfully rode technology wave after wave. From the early days of consoles and personal computers to online games and the latest generation of Sony's PlayStation and Microsoft's Xbox, the company has excelled at creating megahit games loved by millions.

Make no mistake, when you see a state change happening, you usually have an opportunity to participate (as did Blockbuster), but you must change how you think and act fast. You need a high level of adaptability and can't just react defensively.

Software giant Microsoft is a good example: Amazon launched its Amazon Web Services offering in 2002, experienced rapid growth, and was, for quite some time, the dominant force in the market. Under Satya Nadella's leadership, Microsoft flexed its adaptability muscle, doubled down on its cloud infrastructure offering Azure, and developed new product offerings at a breakneck speed. Azure is now the second-largest offering in the marketplace and growing fast. In the process, the company shifted its traditional business model of selling software to one of renting out software-as-a-service; the way you buy Microsoft's flagship Office suite today is not in a box anymore but rather in the form of a monthly subscription. Another old dog learned a new trick and thus stayed relevant.

Christina Nesheva—a former cofounder of the Hive Innovation Unit at ViiV Healthcare, a joint venture between GSK, Pfizer, and Shionogi—points out in my interview with her for the "Disrupt Disruption" podcast: "You can't plan for it—but you can be in the game and prepare to respond and influence how things will play out. It is difficult—if not impossible—to predict the future. But if we engage with the early signals and consider what they mean to us, our business, and our products or services, we can spot the state changes. As much as you can't plan for it, you have to have a system in place; you have to be in the game to have a chance of responding."

During the turn of the millennium, in the early days of eBay Germany, we applied Nesheva's insights daily: by regularly and carefully scanning the data we collected on the business, such as sales and transaction data, user feedback, customer service recordings, and transcripts, my colleagues and I developed an "early warning system" for state changes in our markets. The greatest danger to the business at the time was to miss a new category of items being sold online; imagining it today is hard, but in the year 2000 you would be hard pressed to see anyone selling a used car on the internet. "Cars are being sold at the dealership, or locally from person to person; nobody will sell a car to an unknown buyer across the country" was a commonly referred insight.

By 2001, our early warning system alerted us to the first (admittedly pretty beaten up and thus cheap) cars popping up on the eBay marketplace. A weak signal presented itself. We monitored and supported sales of vehicles on our marketplace with special listing templates and learned as much as possible from the pioneering sellers and buyers. Over time, the weak signal grew stronger and stronger, ending in eBay Motors (the newly formed subdivision of eBay focused solely on facilitating the sale of used cars on the marketplace) being the world's largest marketplace for used vehicles with annual revenues of $11.7 billion in 2021 (Hedges & Company 2022).

DISSECTING STATE CHANGES: THREE PRINCIPLES

As the adage goes: you can't fix what you can't see. To better understand what is happening inside of state changes and, therefore, be prepared to deal with them, let us zoom in on the principles at play. Here we dissect and put them under the microscope to identify what incumbents get wrong—and what we can learn from their mistakes.

As we have already talked about one of the classic disruption stories, Blockbuster, let's pick another: Nokia. And again, we don't intend to pick on Nokia to make fun of them—although Nokia's then CEO Stephen Elop's confession "we didn't do anything wrong, but somehow, we lost" warrants closer inspection as a shining example of a gross misinterpretation of what went on in the market at the time.

Let's step back into the time machine to the decade of relative peace, prosperity, and the emergence of the internet— the nineties. Nokia, a Finnish paper mill founded in 1865, turned rubber boot manufacturer (which you can still buy in specialty stores across Finland), turned telecommunications company, made the first GSM call in the world in 1991. Within seven short years, Nokia established itself as the best-selling mobile phone brand worldwide (Nokia 2022). By 2007 Nokia boasted one billion customers, prompting *Forbes* magazine to put the company's CEO, Olli-Pekka Kallasvuo, on their cover (2007). Kallasvuo looks happy, even smug, holding a banana-shaped cellphone to his ear, with a headline sporting the provocative question "Can Anyone Catch the Cell Phone King?"

Paraphrasing management guru Clayton Christensen again (2013), Nokia perfected the act of sustaining innovation— innovations improving on an existing product in ways customers expect. In other words: Nokia's handsets became a little smaller and a little lighter and the battery life improved, as did the functionality with each new model released.

The same year Kallasvuo crowned the cover of *Forbes* magazine, Nokia introduced the N95—a beautifully crafted aluminum-clad device with a clever dual-sliding mechanism hiding the keypad, a two-camera setup, GPS and mapping capabilities, and a staggering two-week battery life. In many ways, this was the pinnacle of a long series of sustained innovations, all the way from the trusted "brick," the Nokia 1011, which weighed in at nearly half a kilogram, had only twelve hours of standby time, and was introduced fifteen years before the N95 made its debut (Smith 2007).

Apple also introduced the iPhone this year. Four months after Nokia debuted the N95 and two months before it would become widely available, Steve Jobs forever changed how we think about the communication devices in our pockets.

After the dust had settled, the question on everyone's mind was: What the heck is going on at Nokia? How could the cell phone king miss the iPhone? Why did they sing the praises of a small phone with a sliding keyboard when Apple understood consumers wanted big, touch-screen-enabled communication devices? In essence: How did Nokia get disrupted by "the" smartphone?

PRINCIPLE #1:
DISRUPTION IS NEVER ONE FEATURE

And herein lies the problem: the iPhone is not a singular thing ("the" smartphone) but rather a complex and clever combination of many different innovations. It features a large capacitive touch screen, a powerful (and power-hungry) central processing unit (CPU), countless sensors, and a wholly different form factor when compared to a traditional mobile phone.

Nokia had access to the same screen technology, the same chips, and the same sensors but failed to put them together to create something as revolutionary as the iPhone.

Let this sink in for a moment. You will never get disrupted by any one disruptive technology or change. No amount of artificial intelligence, blockchain, genetics, or any other technology will upend your business. Rather, it will be someone combining these technologies in new and interesting ways to create an irresistible product or service.

Stewart Butterfield, founder of the now-ubiquitous and high-growth communication software Slack, put his spin on this principle when he wrote in his seminal blog post and rallying cry for his company, "We Don't Sell Saddles Here" (2014): "The best—maybe the only?—real, direct measure of 'innovation' is a change in human behavior. It is useful to take this way of thinking as definitional: innovation is the sum of change across the whole system, not a thing causing a change in how people behave. No small innovation ever caused a large shift in how people spend their time, and no large one has ever failed to do so."

This brings us to our second principle. Nokia wasn't the only company caught by surprise by the iPhone and drowned in the following tsunami of industry disruption.

PRINCIPLE #2:
YOUR EXISTING SKILLS AND PROCESSES ARE NO LONGER RELEVANT

To this day, I can't listen to the Rolling Stones hit "Start Me Up" and not be reminded of the launch of Windows 95. Bill Gates and his marketing team at Microsoft ruined this song for a whole generation. Only one year later, in 1996, the Redmond-based company introduced a version of its ubiquitous Windows operating system optimized for handheld devices, Windows CE. In 2003, four years before Steve Jobs stepped on stage at Macworld Expo to introduce the iPhone, Microsoft launched Windows Mobile, the successor to Windows CE—an operating system built for mobile devices and smartphones. It turned out to be the portable equivalent of its cousin Windows for PCs, a major force in the then-emerging mobile area.

Shortly after Apple introduced the iPhone in 2007, a CNBC journalist asked Steve Ballmer—Microsoft's then CEO and long-term friend of the company's cofounder Bill Gates—on camera about his initial reaction when he saw the iPhone for the first time. Ballmer broke out into his trademark belly laugh and proclaimed, "Five hundred dollars? Fully subsidized with a plan? That is the most expensive phone in the world. And it doesn't appeal to business customers because it doesn't have a keyboard. Which makes it not a very good email machine" (smugmacgeek 2007).

The video clip has reached cult status on the internet, with dozens of versions circulating on YouTube, many counting millions of views. It is easy to fall in line with the schadenfreude of watching Ballmer whisk the thread of the iPhone away in his typical, slightly maniacal manner—in hindsight, making a fool out of himself as Microsoft shortly after conceded the smartphone market to Apple and Google.

But hindsight is always twenty-twenty. The question thus becomes: What did he see as well as miss in 2007 making him so sure of the imminent failure of the iPhone?

And this is where most of us would have made the same mistake. When you look at Ballmer's response, you realize he is comparing the iPhone to his existing frame of reference: mobile phones à la Nokia and BlackBerry's ubiquitous handheld devices—the "email machine," lovingly referenced as the "Crackberry" due to its addictive nature. The iPhone was indeed the most expensive phone in the world, and it didn't have a keyboard, which made emailing on the device harder than on its rival, the BlackBerry.

But the point is, of course, the iPhone is neither a phone nor a BlackBerry; it is a fully fledged computer in a tiny form factor (and thus the next big stepping stone in the story of mobile communications). The iPhone is as much about being a phone, an email device, a music player, and a camera as it is about anything and everything a clever app developer can imagine.

And this is the reason why the smartphone market could not have been brought about by Nokia or any of its peers: none of them had any experience building computers and writing software for PCs. Nokia's existing skills and processes were in handset manufacturing. All of them became obsolete overnight.

But would the iPhone have been successful by merit of better technology alone? Our third and last principle at play provides the answer.

PRINCIPLE #3:
DISRUPTION ALMOST ALWAYS REACHES A TIPPING POINT AT THE GO-TO-MARKET

Remember buying a cellphone before the iPhone? You walked into a dingy store inside a strip mall with a few select mobile phones on display, chargers and other tchotchkes gathering dust in a broken vitrine, and a grumpy, disinterested twenty-two-year-old behind the counter. His sole interest was to get you on a mobile phone plan with one of the carriers as fast and with as little interaction as possible—as he received a signing bonus from said carriers. The overall experience was akin to buying a car: sleazy salespeople with little to no desire in helping you make a good decision and incentives designed to keep the whole system going.

Compare this with how you bought (and still buy) an iPhone. You walk into a temple of wood, steel, and glass (in other words: the Apple Store), a place so revered some believe it is a place of worship. Once inside, you are greeted by an "Apple Genius." This friendly, well-educated person's sole mission is to make sure you feel welcome and well taken care of. Geniuses don't try to sell you products; instead, they present them to you, let you play with them, ask questions, and—once you make your purchase decision—help set up your new digital friend.

Steve Jobs—and by extension, Apple—understood better than almost anyone else that disruption almost always reaches its make-or-break point at the go-to-market. The company invented a brand-new store concept (heavily prototyped in a secret warehouse location), replaced the salesperson with the "Apple Genius," and hired some of the best retail talents for their stores. The novelty of the device, the comparatively high price point, and the fact Apple had no history in making phones all required a fundamentally different approach to how the product was sold.

We can only speculate, but Apple would doubtfully have been as successful had they chosen the same distribution channels and sales approach as Nokia—and Steve Ballmer would have been right in his assessment that the iPhone is, indeed, "the most expensive phone in the world." The iPhone was the manifestation of a state change requiring a radical rethink of the product and how it was being marketed and sold.

Three major principles are at play when the state changes: disruption originates from the combination and application of technologies, not a singular technology or feature. Once an industry or market enters a phase of disruptive change, the incumbent's existing skills and processes regularly become a hindrance instead of an enabling factor. And lastly, disruption usually happens through a well-executed go-to-market strategy rather than technology per se.

Your company's future depends on your ability to achieve and maintain sustainable relevance—in other words, your ability to play the game of being in business and doing so successfully round after round. Consider the far-reaching implications of technologies and how they will shift your market. Become good at scanning and spotting upcoming state changes. Identify the skills, tools, and processes necessary to compete successfully in the future. Prepare yourself and your organization well ahead of time. Change your go-to-market approach to change the playing field.

Lean into the future, and you will win.

TL;DR

To achieve long-term relevance for your company, consider the following points:

- Evaluate and consider not just a specific technology in isolation but the many ways you can leverage it to satisfy your customer and her job-to-be-done better.
- Investigate the skills, processes, and investments needed to operate successfully in the new state—and make these changes before it is too late.
- Take a holistic view of your customer's experience and your go-to-market strategy, and consider new or different ways to better serve them in the new state.

PART THREE:
TRANSFORM

3

Transforming
the Future

*Transformation means that you lose your original form and are
completely willing to take on new forms. You become an unburnt
pot, as it were. You can no longer be filled with water, but, as
pure clay, you are capable of taking on an endless number of forms.*

—SADHGURU

Transformation might very well be one of the most overused words of our time. Yet, a good reason for it exists: it is
everywhere, necessary, and seldom done well. Four main
challenges stand in the way of successful transformation and
five crucial keys unlock it. They have no specific order nor
weight. They must all be fixed or in place and well executed
for an organization to be successful not just for the short term
but, more importantly, for the long term. As Andy Billings
reiterated in our 2020 conversation: "The goal of the game we
are playing is not innovation nor disruption; it is achieving
sustainable relevance. As such, one doesn't win the game;
one plays to stay in the game and keep playing."

Leaders need to hold on to their good judgment, as they are the ones who know their company inside and out. A good leader understands what their organization can process and digest at any given moment and adjusts the pace and direction accordingly. That being said, we risk running around in circles and chasing our tails if we only listen to well-meant advice and implement it verbatim without the careful transfer and application to our specific circumstances, setup, capabilities, and culture.

To get us started on our transformation journey, consider the sage advice presented by a young executive at Pearson, the world's leading learning company, when she presented her plan for the future in front of an auditorium at a posh San Francisco Bay Area hotel packed with high-level company executives and advisors (including yours truly). Gleaming lights highlighted her face, her PowerPoint deck projected on a large screen, ready to go. She leaned forward and started her presentation: "It is not complicated. It is just hard."

Let's explore.

3.1

Faults
(The Four Horsemen)

Change is not necessary because survival is not mandatory.
—W. EDWARDS DEMING

War, famine, pestilence, death—these are humanity's punishments from the New Testament's prophetic book of Revelations. Turned into a famous woodcut by artist Albrecht Dürer, the four horsemen are believed to represent the tribulations of men, or as historian Edward B. Elliott points out, the "general subject is the decline and fall, after a previous prosperous era, of the Empire of Heathen Rome" (1862).

The picture is dramatic and evocative, yet feels appropriate when talking about the decline of once-leading industry titans such as the aforementioned Nokia, Blockbuster, and Kodak, as well as the possibility of this fate happening to today's leading companies. Innosight has discovered that the last couple of years have seen a drastic decline in the average time a company stays on the Fortune 500 index down to fifteen to twenty years in this decade, with around twenty companies exiting the index each year (Viguerie et al. 2021).

In our work with incumbent organizations worldwide, regardless of industry, geography, or size, we encounter four common challenges organizations face when transforming their business and operations. We have come to call them "the four horsemen."

Let me introduce you to the four horsemen of failed transformation.

THE WHITE HORSE: FEAR OF CANNIBALIZATION

Our first horseman, riding on his shiny white horse, is common and typically better understood inside organizations. Still, it is one many companies stumble over: the fear of cannibalization.

Your organization enjoys stable market share, predictable margins, growth, and profitability—resulting in a world in which, to borrow the words of Jorge Paulo Lemann, "all you needed to care about is being very efficient, and you'd be okay" (Samor 2018). Yet, often with the rise of a new state comes a change to your business model—not just in how you do things but also in how you charge for your products and services and run your business.

In *The Innovator's Dilemma*, Clayton Christensen showed disruptive change frequently emerges from a new state offering lower margins, smaller addressable markets, and thus lessened profitability and revenue potential compared to the current state (2013). Which brings many leaders to ask, "Why would I want to do this and thus cannibalize my existing business?"

The answer is, of course: if you don't do it, someone else will. But the reality of this question isn't quite as clear cut. State changes are easy to spot with hindsight but can be opaque in the moment. Overcoming the organizational and psychological inertia of shedding invested resources, reputation, and energy is hard. Balancing a compassionate understanding of existing commitments with the ruthless necessity to stay current, much less ahead, of one's markets is complex. And companies must explain themselves to their boards and shareholders; telling them you will make less money doing the new thing is a tough pill to swallow.

And so, you don't do it—until, typically, a new entrant, unencumbered by a long history, comes along and develops and therefore disrupts the market which could have been yours. The result is a company moving instantly from leader to follower—not able to control the game and being forced to play by the rules of others. The irony is, of course, we all should know better by now. The reality, though, is greed and short-term thinking still reign supreme in the corporate world.

The stock trading platform Robinhood, founded in 2013, became a cultural and commercial phenomenon by offering free stock trades to its customers. Millennials and Gen Z flocked to the company's snazzy mobile app, often making their very first stock trades on the new platform, turning Robinhood itself into a publicly traded company with a $30 billion market cap on its first day of trading.

Forty years before Robinhood made its debut, Charles Schwab brought cheap, accessible stock trading to the masses and, in 2005, eliminated all account service and order-handling fees. Yet the company failed, until recently, to counter Robinhood's free trades and thus lost significant market and mind share for next-generation traders. They would have been able to offer free trading, but the company made substantial amounts of money with their fixed-price trades and thus was stuck with the first horseman: the fear of cannibalization.

Founder and former chairman and CEO of Silicon Valley-based accounting software giant Intuit—and quite possibly one of Silicon Valley's best leaders—Scott Cook's words ring true as an important warning: "Success is a powerful thing. It tends to make companies stupid, and they become less and less innovative" (Nisen 2013).

THE RED HORSE: THE EXPENSIVE BAGGAGE YOU CARRY

A close cousin, with subtle yet critical differences, is the red horse—"the expensive baggage you carry" fallacy. Similar in result to its cousin, the white horse (the fear of cannibalization), the red horse shows up slightly differently.

Every incumbent organization has existing capital and operational expenditures, CapEx and OpEx for short—buildings and machines leased or bought, software deployed, and people hired. This existing infrastructure serves a company well, allowing organizations to operate effectively and efficiently. And when improved products or services are being created, it ensures these will benefit from all the optimizations that have come before, allowing the incumbent to cement their position in the market further.

But when states change, existing CapEx and OpEx can quickly become a hard liability to shed. Capital investments need to be amortized (or written off), and the change in workforce capabilities and expertise often occurs faster than the organization's ability to re-skill or acquire new talent. The latter point proves particularly thorny, as talent with the required new skills is in short supply (which creates an opportunity for smart re- and upskilling, as we will see when we get to the fixes in the following chapters).

On the other hand, while new entrants do not benefit from a long history of CapEx and OpEx investments, they also don't have to deal with outdated technologies or employees in urgent need of up- and re-skilling once the new state rolls around. One's legacy becomes one's burden.

On March 14, 2006, online retailer Amazon publicly launched the now ubiquitous Amazon Web Services platform by introducing the Simple Storage Service (S3) (Hargrove n.d.). This ushered in the era of cloud computing. Only a few years later, with Amazon launching dozens of new services on its cloud infrastructure, the company established itself firmly as the leader in the space.

Around that time, I sat down with the chief technology officer of a larger European private bank. Over dinner, we discussed the merits of cloud-based infrastructure, these services' price competitiveness, ease of use, and near-infinite scalability. After much agreement on the merit and value of moving to the cloud, over traditional German (and particularly rich) Black Forest cherry cake, I asked when the bank would move (parts of) their infrastructure to the cloud. The CTO put his dessert fork down, took a long sip of his coffee, and responded: "We won't. We just invested in a new data center which cost us north of $50 million, and by god, we will need to use the asset."

This is the challenge with the red horse: despite better knowledge and judgment, incumbents put themselves at a disadvantage as they feel obligated (often for good reasons) to use their existing CapEx and OpEx, even if it means the company must compete on the uneven playing field it has created for itself. Legacy often is a huge asset if you operate in a mode of sustaining innovation. It can turn into your biggest liability when you find yourself in a disruptive innovation situation.

THE BLACK HORSE: AUTOIMMUNE REACTIONS

Nearly all organisms have developed a highly evolved and incredibly effective network of biological processes protecting them from disease—the immune system. It detects and responds to a wide variety of pathogens, from viruses to parasitic worms, as well as cancer cells and objects such as wood splinters, distinguishing them from the organism's healthy tissue (Johns Hopkins Medicine n.d.).

Similarly, companies evolve to develop their version of an immune system. At first, every startup or project within an established organization is in discovery and exploration mode. One tries many things, iterates, tests, and creates prototypes and minimally viable products. Hopefully, and often after many iterations and sleepless nights, one moves from this initial phase of exploration and innovation to the stage of having achieved product/market fit. The product or service finds its audience and satisfies its market demand. Silicon Valley legend Marc Andreessen succinctly summarized this: "The only thing that matters is getting to product/market fit" (2007).

Once product/market fit has been reached, the organization starts developing an immune system—a system protecting the venture from competitors and other market participants. Over time, immune systems grow more robust and can eventually calcify. Organizations start hiring people who excel at defending the status quo to strengthen their immune defenses. All this is good, but every so often, the immune system turns on itself and develops autoimmune reactions. In organisms, an autoimmune reaction or disease is a condition arising from an abnormal immune response to a functioning body part (Watson 2022). In the world of organizations, this expresses itself when the immune system defends the status quo from the outside world as well as new ideas from the inside. The telltale comment in any meeting is someone saying, "this is not how we do things here" or "we already tried that; it doesn't work."

I've lost count of how many times I've battled with autoimmune reactions in organizations I have worked for—including world-leading companies such as Google, where the black horse often hides as "culture" (as in "this is how we do things here at Google") or is buried deep in intellectual argument.

Your organization's immune system is essential and necessary for survival, and every organization has one. The issue arises when the immune system turns on itself, attacks new and fresh ideas, reverts to institutionalized memory of previously failed experiments, and prevents the organization from evolving. Become creative and develop ways to immunize yourself from autoimmune attacks. One of our clients loves to hand out sachets of Vitamin C every time someone in a meeting reflexively says "no." What started as a tongue-in-cheek joke became a powerful reminder not to let the immune system run amok.

THE PALE HORSE: THE TIME HORIZON FALLACY

At the turn of the millennium, consulting firm McKinsey introduced the "Three Time Horizons" framework through Mehrdad Baghai, Stephen Coley, and David White's book, *The Alchemy of Growth* (2000). The idea is simple, compelling, and makes sense—which explains why the model made its way into the toolbox of every strategist and consultant around the world. McKinsey urged companies to invest not only in the short-term ("Time Horizon 1" or, in the vernacular of consulting firm EY, "Now")—which all companies do, as otherwise they wouldn't be able to deliver their products and services to their clients—but also in the intermediary future ("Time Horizon 2" or "Next"—typically two to five years out) and the long-term ("Time Horizon 3" or "Beyond"—anything beyond five years; often this is research and development, shortened as R&D). With this framework, the firm highlighted one of the crucial challenges companies face: the duality of short- and long-term.

More than twenty years on, some fallacies present themselves when applying this model to one's business. Geoffrey Moore, the author of a series of seminal books in the disruption canon, including the cult classic *Crossing the Chasm* (1991), points to three related fallacies we encounter daily in our practice with clients.

The first encounter with the pale horse happens when the brave leader of a Time Horizon 2 initiative (as a quick reminder: they work on a project which is two to five years out from the market) meets their Horizon 1-centric leader and asks for additional resources to scale up their project.

On a hot summer's day, Beth, a young, energetic leader working on a new language learning app for one of our clients in the education space, met with her Horizon 1-centric leader (who shall go unnamed to protect the innocent) to present her idea, demonstrate a working prototype, and discuss the business plan for the new product. Upon talking her boss through the details, a bead of sweat dropping off her brow (she blamed the weather), her boss did what most Horizon 1 leaders do. He asked for metrics fitting into his existing frame of reference: "When will we have 100,000 users on the app?" and "When will you make us money with this product?" Operating squarely in Horizon 2, Beth responded with a nearly invisible shrug of her shoulders and a somewhat unusual quiet voice: "I don't know. Nobody knows, as nobody has ever done this before."

Her comment yielded a predictable response; the request for resources was denied. The first of the Three Time Horizon fallacies strikes: the application of Horizon 1 thinking and metrics to Horizon 2 initiatives.

Horizon 2 leaders eventually wizen up. As someone who has spent his whole career working in the exciting and sometimes daunting world of Horizon 2, I can tell you what happens (and happened in this case as well): you start to learn to speak the language of your Horizon 1 leader. Beth threw herself into the challenge and produced the Excel spreadsheets and PowerPoint slides demonstrating exponential growth— well knowing this was all wishful thinking which might or might not be true, as nobody could know: the essence of Horizon 2 is that it is inherently unknown. But so it goes, and eventually, she received her resources. Alas, a moment of joyous working on (and in) the future is often followed by fallacy number two.

The moment the organization's core falls on hard times—revenues decline, customer sentiment shifts, or a global pandemic disrupts life as we know it—Horizon 1 loves going to Horizon 2 to ask for its resources back. The argument is simple, irrefutable, and shortsighted: Horizon 2 doesn't generate revenue. All of which is, of course, upside down. Horizon 1, as much as it might generate the needed cash flow, is the present and the past; Horizon 2 is the future. Yet, we frequently plunder the resources from our future, which sadly happened to our young heroine. With a shift in the company's market, the organization found itself in a cash flow pinch and ripped the guts out of the new project by reassigning its team to other parts of the company. Maybe even more tragically, Beth left the company after being frustrated by the whole experience.

And lastly, as Geoffrey Moore passionately advocates for, you can only bring a single major project from your R&D team (and thus Horizon 3) through Horizon 2 into the here and now, your Horizon 1. The moment you try to bring multiple projects forward at the same time, you confuse your market, overload your systems and infrastructure, and establish competing priorities for your sales team—all surefire recipes for disaster.

I had the enormous fortune to work alongside Geoffrey Moore during my time at Mozilla, the nonprofit organization behind the Firefox web browser. At the time, Mozilla tried to introduce a mobile phone operating system (Firefox OS) alongside a set of web services, such as the identity system Persona, while maintaining its position in the web browser market. In essence, we had a well-established Horizon 1 product, Firefox, with 500 million users worldwide and multiple initiatives pushing through Horizon 2.

Moore urged us to reconsider our approach and timing—and relayed a story from his work with Apple, where he was a personal advisor to Steve Jobs. When Apple introduced the iPhone in 2007, its bigger cousin, the iPad, was essentially ready (the concepts and prototypes for the iPad even predate the iPhone). Introducing both a smartphone and a tablet simultaneously would have significantly reduced the impact either of those devices would have had in the market and would have provided substantial managerial challenges inside the company regarding focus and resource allocation. After introducing the iPhone and asking if Apple would build a tablet, Jobs quipped that Apple wouldn't make a tablet, tablets are a dumb idea, and the future is the iPhone. In essence, Jobs lied to keep both his customers and internal teams focused on one thing, and one thing only: the revolutionary iPhone. When Apple introduced the iPad to an excited audience three years later, Jobs reversed his stance to say the tablet project was "the most important thing I've ever done" (Arrington 2010). Jobs knew that the market, his customers, and his company could only handle one major innovation at a time and did everything he could to shield internal and external stakeholders through the singular focus on the iPhone and, later, the iPad.

Years later, when asked what Apple's approach to innovation was, Jobs summarized the insight he had learned from Moore succinctly: "We have one team working on one thing" (Moore 2015).

NAME YOUR HORSEMEN

The four horsemen love to travel together and often bring fellow travelers, resulting in a fifth (and sixth) horseman. Take some time to map the four horsemen to your organization; I have yet to find a company where they don't ring true. Identify their companions, as more than just four riders are certainly galloping through your land.

Only when we can name and tame the horsemen and overcome the faults in our organizations can we tackle transformation successfully.

TL;DR

To rein in the four horsemen, consider the following points:

- Treat the possibility of cannibalizing your existing business as an opportunity, not a threat. If you don't do it, someone else will.
- Take a hard look at your assets—both CapEx and OpEx—and separate those which will serve you in the future from those which won't. Shed, repurpose, or upgrade the latter ones.
- Map out your organization's immune system and develop early warning and defense systems for signs of the immune system attacking the organization itself.
- Create processes and key performance indicators for your Time Horizon 2 projects. Once in place, create ways to protect these projects from the rest of the organization.

3.2
Fixes

The only way to make sense out of change is to plunge into it, move with it, and join the dance.

—ALAN WATTS

Computer, console, and online gaming giant Electronic Arts (EA) operates in an industry famously eating its young. Founded nearly forty years ago by visionary game designer Trip Hawkins, EA not only managed to stay relevant throughout numerous state changes in the industry but continues to innovate at a blistering pace. EA is a titan in the global gaming market from early PC gaming to consoles and now internet-enabled and cloud-based gaming. With a market cap of more than $35 billion and a stock price soaring tenfold in the last ten years (Yahoo Finance 2022), the company has shown an old dog can truly learn many new tricks.

During our 2020 conversation, EA's Andy Billings reflected on his company's approach to innovation and disruption. After a series of thoughtful comments on the strategies, tactics, and processes his team deploys, Billings went silent, deep in thought, then asked of himself and his company:

Is it really possible to be planful, thoughtful, effective, well-organized, and linear in managing disruptive change? When you talk to the people on the front lines, they will tell you it doesn't look like what it is being described as in the books.

Having been on the front lines of innovation, having worked on countless Horizon 2 initiatives, and having read any book and article I could find helping me with the challenges of managing disruptive change, I believe Andy is right. Most of what we talk about in the books makes perfect sense on paper and in the boardroom but is far removed from the reality on the ground.

And so began my search for the ingredients making disruptive change work: over the next two and a half years, we conducted in-depth interviews with more than 250 practitioners—the very people Billings referred to as "the people on the front lines" of disruptive change. We started each discussion with a simple question: "What do you do to make innovation, disruption, and thus transformation work?"

We codified these insights and cross-referenced them with the literature. From the popular canon on innovation and disruption to the latest academic research, we tested our insights extensively with our clients, refined them over and over again, and validated them with organizations ranging from small- and medium-sized businesses to Fortune 500 companies and thought leaders in the field.

Ultimately, we cracked the code to successful transformation—and you can count the fixes on a single hand.

FIVE KEYS TO UNLOCK YOUR TRANSFORMATION

In this section, we will dig deep into the five keys which have unlocked successful transformation for leaders at organizations including telecommunication company Telefónica's Alpha innovation unit; 115-year-old German steel manufacturing powerhouse Klöckner & Co; the Wikimedia Foundation, which brought the world the online encyclopedia Wikipedia; DIY retail giant Lowe's; software leader SAP; the World Food Program; and the consulting firm EY. In addition, you will meet and learn from globally renowned thought leaders from organizations like Massachusetts Institute of Technology (MIT) and Stanford's Hasso Plattner Institute of Design—commonly known as the d.school—as well as leaders at highly innovative and disruptive small- and medium-sized businesses from all around the world.

What all these leaders have in common is they led (often multiple times and for prolonged periods of time) successful transformation initiatives—not from a corner office on the twenty-fifth floor of a glass-clad high rise, but deep in the trenches of disruptive change, right where the action happens. Each one of those leaders emphasized specific keys which proved to be particularly relevant in their respective circumstances, and noted all the other keys as foundational for their sustained success in transforming (and transforming again) their businesses. Each might use different language to describe the keys and put their spin on them—but the five keys show up consistently in their respective work.

Successful transformations start from first-principles thinking, incorporate agile principles across the whole organization, and manage the tension between the core and the edge of the organization. Leaders exhibit a set of specific leadership traits and focus energy on up- and reskilling their workforce. In summary: five keys unlock your ability to spot and ride the waves of state changes and create sustainable relevance for the long run.

Note: I don't believe in dogma. None of our interviewees presented their comments as the Truth (with a capital "T") but rather as underlying fundamental insights that require a careful application to one's circumstances. Each company operates in different industries and markets. They work with different people, approaches to running the company, and cultures (both inside the organization and in the market in which it operates). Cookie-cutter approaches and dogmatic views don't work; your job (should you choose to accept it) is to take what we learned and make it work for your organization.

This is your company and your journey. You know your business better than any outsider ever could. Learn from those who have successfully navigated transformation, ask the (usually) hard questions, be honest with yourself, and make the learnings from this book your own.

A bit of a fair warning before we get started: nobody likes change (especially when it is done *to* them). And, certainly, nobody likes disruptive change; the markets don't like it as they tend to focus on the short term, and your people don't like it as they fear losing their bonuses and jobs. And so, theoretically, you will have everyone against you. In this context, we must remind ourselves this is not a "from/to proposition." It is not something you go through and come out at the other end, where it will be peaceful and calm (again). Instead, it is never going to stop. Thus, what we need to learn as leaders and as organizations is not how to get *through* disruption, but how to live *in* disruption, to be continuously changing, adapting, and evolving. Disruption is a polarity to be managed, not a problem to be solved. Too little and you are in trouble, as you become stale; too much and your company spins out of control.

As Kyle Nel, whom we will meet again later, quips: "You don't want to be overwhelmed, nor underwhelmed; you just want to be 'whelmed.'"

But, of course, change is not an option, but an imperative. Let's get to work.

Key 1: First-Principles Thinking

Give me but one firm spot on which to stand, and I will move the earth.

—ARCHIMEDES

What do business tycoon Elon Musk and philosopher Aristotle have in common? No, this is not a trick question. More than 2,300 years ago, the Greek philosopher Aristotle defined a foundational way of thinking by encouraging his students, who included Alexander the Great, to argue up from "the first basis from which a thing is known" (*Metaphysics* 1013a14-15). Over the centuries, Aristotle's "first-principles thinking" became the basis of the scientific method—deriving from and building upon what we know is fundamentally true. Meanwhile, mental shortcuts were established in many other parts of society—including modern-day businesses—to speed up information processing and decision making.

First-principles thinking is experiencing a renaissance these days. George Constantinescu, chief transformation officer at Canadian engineering, logistics, and energy company ATCO, shares not only his heritage with the Greek philosopher Aristotle but also his ability for deep thought. During a long conversation we held over Zoom during the COVID-19 pandemic lockdown, rain hammering the windows of my makeshift home office, he remarked, "The part of the journey we are all on is to discipline ourselves enough to take the time and do the hard work to figure out what the actual question we should actually be asking is—and answering it."

The same sentiment showed up in essentially every interview we did. Transformation, and thus innovation and disruption, starts with asking the hard question of what we actually know to be true and then arguing up from there, be it the truth about our customers' needs or how things are being created, made, and sold. Instead of engaging in the hard, arduous work of arguing up from the irrefutable truth of the individual components making up a solution, modern-day decision-makers rely on assumptions, conjectures, and proxies to make fast decisions.

Aristotle's ideas were pulled into the spotlight when Tesla's founder and serial entrepreneur Elon Musk described the approach in an interview with Silicon Valley celebrity Kevin Rose (innomind 2013). Musk responded, when asked about Tesla and the reason he built his own battery factory, "It is important to reason from first principles rather than by analogy. Arguing by analogy is mentally easier; arguing from first principles is a physics way of looking at the world. By boiling things down to the most fundamental truths and asking: 'What do we know for sure is true?' we can then reason up from there."

Musk applied this way of thinking when he needed to acquire large amounts of lithium-ion battery packs for his electric vehicles. Tesla's suppliers kept telling him they were expensive (to the tune of $600 per kilowatt/hour) and they would always be that way. Instead of accepting this view, Musk challenged his team to argue from first principles and identify the raw ingredients which make one of these batteries: cobalt, nickel, aluminum, carbon, and polymers. By looking at this fundamental truth and researching the price for the raw materials, his team realized the bill for the raw materials only amounted to eighty dollars, a fraction of the cost for an assembled battery. This insight led to the creation of the Gigafactory, Musk's battery manufacturing facility.

Even if you don't have the billions of dollars it takes to build your own version of the Gigafactory, gaining a fundamental, first-principles-based understanding allows you to be a shrewd negotiator and strategist.

First-principles thinking is the bedrock for every innovator we interviewed. It is the first step on a team's journey toward transformation and identifying and preparing yourself for upcoming state changes. As science fiction author Jeff VanderMeer has one of his characters in his book *Authority* (2014) remark: "Because our minds process information almost solely through analogy and categorization, we are often defeated when presented with something that fits no category and lies outside of the realm of our analogies. A circle looks at a square and sees a badly made circle."

In our conversations, leaders frequently brought up three distinct yet connected approaches to first-principles thinking—pointing out how all three need to be used to gain a holistic view of the challenge, opportunity, and possible solutions. In essence (and in the words of Maurice Conti, former head of Moonshots at Telefónica Alpha): "The most important thing is having a crystal-clear understanding of the problem you're trying to solve. [This] sounds easy, yet is remarkably hard to do, as we vastly underestimate the difficulty, importance, and value of achieving brilliant clarity."

FIRST PRINCIPLES FROM THE INSIDE-OUT

"When you make paper clips, it is all too easy to become a paper clip company—striving to become the world's best in making paper clips." Rodolfo Rosini, lead tech coach at Conception X, started our conversation about first principles and, specifically, being strongly dialed in with the customer's needs with this crucial warning.

But when the market shifts, the states change, and you realize the world is moving on from paper clips, it is often incredibly hard to shift from making paper clips to getting back in touch with the starting point of your journey—your customers' needs.

The moral of Rosini's warning: don't be a paper clip company, but one which solves its customers' jobs to be done (which might, for the time being, be through paper clips).

We like to ask our clients' executives a provocative question: How much time did you spend with your customer last week? Not wining and dining—but on the ground, observing, asking questions, and gaining a fundamental understanding of their needs? The answer tends to be … zero.

As mentioned before, to get started with first-principles thinking, focus on identifying the "capital T" truth about what you know for sure to be true. This can be the physical constituent parts of what we are building (as was the case in the Musk example earlier) or can be anchored in a fundamental understanding of your customers' needs and wants (their jobs to be done). Once done, layer into this analysis your organization's inherent abilities, strengths, and weaknesses. The overlap between product, market need, and your organization's capabilities provides you with a clear picture of your opportunities.

Starting in 2006, Harvard Business School professor Michael Porter and his colleague Nitin Nohria tracked how CEOs spend their day. Sixty thousand hours of tracked time later, they found CEOs, on average, spend a measly 3 percent of their total working time with customers—a number which is topped even by the 5 percent they spend with consultants (Porter 2018). In a world of rapid state changes, where understanding a customer's jobs to be done is paramount, this doesn't bode well.

This is inside-out thinking—applying a first-principles lens to the internal side of your business.

FOLLOW ME HOME

Time travel with me to the year 1983. Toto hit number one in the charts with "Africa"—a song that's truly had many lives since then. The internet as we know it came to be that year, and the world's first mobile cellular telephone call was made. If you bought a personal computer that year (likely an Apple IIe or maybe an IBM PC-compatible machine), you might have found yourself leaving the computer store with your shiny new PC in your shopping cart, ready to be loaded into the trunk of your car, being approached by a nicely dressed young man who introduced himself as "Scott from Intuit." Scott—that is, Scott Cook, the founder and CEO of software company Intuit—would have told you about his new accounting software, called Quicken, and asked if he could give you a free copy and watch you install it.

And so, Intuit established their "Follow Me Home" (FMH) tradition. To this day, Intuit employees regularly spend time with their customers—not asking them to come to Intuit's headquarters in Mountain View, California, and sit down in their nice cafeteria under the Californian sun, sip some flavored sparkling water imported from some exotic-sounding town in Europe, and enjoy one of the many free snacks, but following their customers home.

Inspired by biologist and nature documentary filmmaker Sir David Attenborough, Intuit's employees observe their study subjects in their natural habitat. They carefully avoid any interference, just taking in everything their customers do—from their little annoyances, the small hacks they deploy to make something work just the way they want, and the things they do manually despite having their computer in front of them, to the moments when they could do something with their computer but don't, as they might not even know it is possible.

This practice has been expanded and refined since those early days of Cook talking to PC users in the parking lot of the local computer store—with the most important element of a successful FMH being the ability to walk into a session "with no assumptions or expectations on how the interviewee will use the products or what set of challenges they face on a daily basis" (Flowers 2021). By doing so, you allow yourself to "be surprised" and avoid applying preconceived notions and biases to the situation or seeking confirmation for assumptions you hold.

In our interview for the Disrupt Disruption podcast, Amy Radin, a Fortune 100 executive and strategist, recalls deploying a customer-centric first-principles view at a life sciences technology company and adds some important insights. The company was strongly sales and product driven. With a looming state change on the horizon, Radin set out to better understand the company's customers and their jobs to be done.

She needed a few months to convince the head of sales it was "okay for me to talk to our customers." After finally receiving the go-ahead, Radin discovered she was handed a carefully curated list of eight customers she was allowed to talk to. The list consisted of the company's salespeople believing they "own the customer," and they didn't want her to cause too much trouble. Radin persevered, conducting her interviews and "follow-me-homes," and recalls in our conversation, "It was like holding up a mirror to the company's face; here is how your customers see you, why they really hire you, and what their real challenges are."

As a result, the company added a new business line, changed others, revamped its sales strategy, and rethought its brand strategy, as most of its most significant brand assets weren't even present in its marketing materials.

"Are you really listening to your customers?" became Radin's starting question for any new endeavor; it should be yours as well.

THE INVERSE: FIRST PRINCIPLES FROM THE OUTSIDE IN

Flipping your perspective is not only good relationship advice. While the inside-out perspective is firmly anchored in the here and now, an outside-in perspective opens you up to the future. This lens inverts the view from an internal perspective. Instead of asking what you know to be fundamentally true about the things in your sphere of direct influence (your customers, your product, and your organization), in the outside-in approach to first-principles thinking, you ask what the known changes in the world are. By looking at demographic, environmental, and political changes, you can predict the future with a high(er) degree of certainty.

Lisa Kay Solomon, professor at Stanford's d.school, likes to point out if your target demographic is, for example, thirty-to forty-year-old women, you can precisely know how that demographic is shifting over the next ten years by simply looking at the women who are in their twenties to thirties today. We often refer to these trends as "megatrends"—the inevitable, longer-term shifts which will define our world in the future.

Solomon likes to further separate the elements of this future into those which are fixed (i.e., 100 percent certain, demographics being an example here), and those which have some level of uncertainty but clear directionality. For the latter, climate change comes to mind—an inevitable change to our environment with considerable ramifications for society and business, yet one where a level of uncertainty exists as to how it will play out precisely. Adding nuance to the analysis allows you to create scenarios within each megatrend, further exploring possible futures.

An expert in looking at systems, their surrounding environments, and their impact on businesses, Hannah Tucker, the founder of Balance Point Ventures, applies a holistic framework to her work. Tucker does so by considering both the social and environmental conditions, as well as information and technological capabilities to her outside-in thinking, in a framework she summarized as "considering both conditions and capabilities."

Tucker mentioned one of her former clients, a beef processing company, as an example. She started with the direct impact of climate change on the viability of growing livestock—land which becomes unusable for cattle to roam and feed on due to changes in average temperatures and rainfall. She continued her analysis by looking at the social aspects of livestock being a significant contributor to the climate crisis—and thus, potential consumer backlash. By applying her framework, she looked even further upstream to identify challenges in the production of feed for livestock (the climate crisis plays another significant role here) having strong ripple effects down the value chain.

Considering the high degree of certainty we have about those impacts, it behooves companies in this business to apply first-principles thinking on an outside-in basis to ensure adaptability and resilience. And it is not just threats but opportunities we can identify by using this lens to peek into the future.

As we said before: your job as a leader is to spot the waves of the future and ensure you stand upright on the surfboard that is your business when those waves crest. Companies and their leaders are well served by creating an as-complete-as-possible inventory of those outside-in changes and incorporating them into their strategy. Often, you will find state changes prefaced by inevitable shifts to the macro landscape we operate in—making those state changes much easier to predict and prepare for.

Just like surfing on the coast of Hawaii becomes easier the more you learn to read the ocean and get out on your board, spotting state changes becomes second nature the more you do it. Fostering expertise and intimate knowledge of the relevant externalities to your business requires discipline, resources, and continued effort.

Go grab your surfboard and get out there.

LEARNING FROM PARALLEL WORLDS

Maybe you need to be an award-winning filmmaker to discover a third, unique perspective to gain insights into the problem, opportunity, and solution. This method was first described to us by Alvaro Delgado Aparicio, the cofounder,

CEO, and chief innovation officer of BREIN, Grupo BRECA's innovation hub. Grupo BRECA is one of the largest companies in Peru—a conglomerate spanning primary industries such as fishing all the way to mining, healthcare, and financial services. Alvaro is also the director of the BAFTA-nominated feature film *Retablo*—and thus brings a unique perspective to first-principles thinking.

In addition to an inside-out and outside-in perspective, Aparicio looks for fundamental truths in other adjacent fields which translate into the primary domain of his businesses. Working with a team of data scientists at BREIN developing new products for Grupo BRECA's banking unit and anticipating an upcoming state change in how younger consumers expect to bank in the future, Aparicio discovered a lack of customer-centricity and empathy in the team. The BREIN team had mapped the insight-out-validated customer expectations, needs, and wants and created a concise formulation of the jobs to be done. Mapping these to megatrends, particularly shifting consumer demographics and technological breakthroughs, the team was able to formulate a clear vision of the technological nature of the upcoming state change. Yet, the team lacked an empathetic understanding of their customers' desires.

Looking at parallel worlds, which offer essential insights and learnings into the behaviors of the target demographic, Aparicio identified the hospitality sector as particularly fitting: hospitality thrives on innovative approaches to customer-centricity. Consequently, Aparicio's team worked alongside hotel and restaurant staff to learn from this sector's approach to meeting customer needs. The experience resulted in crucial insights which shaped the specific mechanics as well as the user experience of the new product.

"Parallel worlds" is a powerful concept enriching typical approaches to first-principles-based thinking—and points toward a vital insight Lisa Kay Solomon shared with us:

- Look for multiple perspectives: seek viewpoints different from yours to avoid biases.
- Take varying vantage points to identify blind spots.
- Treat your insights as hypotheses to be tested, not beliefs to be protected.

FIRST PRINCIPLES SUMMARIZED

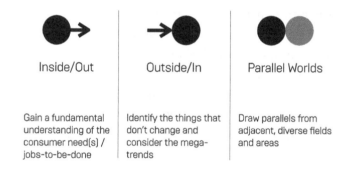

Inside/Out	Outside/In	Parallel Worlds
Gain a fundamental understanding of the consumer need(s) / jobs-to-be-done	Identify the things that don't change and consider the mega-trends	Draw parallels from adjacent, diverse fields and areas

Three Approaches to First-Principles Thinking

Every single leader we talked to in our research started their transformation journey from first principles. Take it from Rick Smith, founder and CEO of Axon. His publicly traded company has a singular focus on "making the bullet obsolete" by creating products such as the Taser stun gun. After his team conceptualized Axon's digital evidence storage platform for law enforcement by looking at parallel worlds, Smith went on to build it by operating from first principles:

We looked at what was happening in other industries with the move to cloud-based infrastructure and wanted to create a digital-native, cloud-based platform to allow public safety personnel to gather and store evidence. In the process, we received strong pushback—arguments such as "this is illegal," "the evidence has to be stored at the police department," etc. By applying a first-principles-based approach, we quickly learned the customer objections were, in fact, rooted in fear about the system's security—an objection we could quickly overcome by pointing out cloud-based infrastructure benefits from a much more robust security model than the crummy PC being found in a remote police station.

Many of us jump to a solution too quickly. George Constantinescu urges us to slow down, even if it's just a little bit: "Many conversations tend to lead with solutions—quite often the specific solution promoted by a provider. Frequently these end up being simplifications, even oversimplifications, of the things we really ought to be considering. Questions such as: What is the purpose of our work? What do our customers truly want? How do they interact with us and our products and services? How can we provide those more efficiently? Once you start asking those questions, you discover there is a broad range of possible answers—and then the question becomes: How can we fulfill the job to be done for the highest number of people, doing the highest amount of good, most economically, and in the fairest way possible?"

Start your transformation journey by inquiring, "What do we know to be fundamentally true?" and construct your argument up from there.

TL;DR

To become an expert in first-principles thinking, consider the following points:

- Start by defining what you know to be fundamentally true and argue up from there: (1) Identify and define your current assumptions. (2) Break down the problem into its fundamental principles. (3) Create new solutions from scratch.
- Look at the opportunity space through the three lenses of first-principles thinking: inside-out, outside-in, and parallel worlds.
- Consider creating your own Follow Me Home program; the approach yields surprising insights and results.
- Most importantly: prioritize gaining fundamental, not superficial, insights into all relevant aspects of your business.

3.2.2

Key 2: Agile Everywhere

Doing things at high speed, that's the best defense against the future.

—JEFF BEZOS

"Agile" isn't new. Since the 1960s, researchers and practitioners have run studies, gained insights, and developed methodologies to better understand and harness the potential for human creativity and creativity-enhancing methods.

The 1980s gave rise to human-centered design and design-centered business management, placing the human front and center of an organization's initiative. In 1990, IDEO—the pioneering design consultancy which went on to popularize the ideas encapsulated by design thinking—was founded. In 2001, a group of software developers and product managers published the Agile Software Development manifesto, codifying, for the first time, the agile development process—and introducing the concept of the "minimal viable product" (MVP) (Beck et al. 2001).

Eric Ries, who ten years later published the seminal guide-book *The Lean Startup*, defined an MVP as "that version of a new product which allows a team to collect the maximum amount of validated learning about customers with the least effort" (2011). Since then, "agile" has moved from the canon of buzzwords to a well-established business practice.

By now, agile approaches have been around for decades and had plenty of time to mature. Stated simply: we know how to do this. Yet, we still seem to not do it across the enterprise.

Aside from having defined the problem space and possible solutions from the ground up using first-principles thinking, our interviewees consistently brought up the importance of key two: Agile Everywhere—specifically, your organization's extensive use of agile processes.

When we talk about "agile," we don't refer to the specific forms of agile development processes commonly used in software development, such as scrum, but rather a broader application of agile methodologies to your business processes. Take, for example, the way most organizations run their marketing: instead of quick iterations, running lots of small and cheap tests, and incorporating the results into consecutive versions of a marketing campaign, we still spend millions of dollars on marketing agencies, believing the marketing genius of New York's famous Madison Avenue is alive and kicking.

Agility has its roots in complexity theory; an agile approach acknowledges the complexity and one's inability to communicate all requirements upfront clearly and comprehensively.

In the fifteenth State of Agile Report (digital.ai 2022), practitioners of agile methodologies confirmed the business benefits of applying agile methods: better management of changing priorities, increased visibility of the status of a project, better alignment, quicker time to market, and increased productivity. It goes without saying these are highly desirable factors any company seeks in today's business environment of increasing uncertainty and complexity.

The agile approach can be best summarized as "the ability to create and respond to change. It is a way of dealing with, and ultimately succeeding in, an uncertain and turbulent environment" (Agile Alliance 2022). Chris Yeh described the approach in my conversations with him as "the pursuit of rapid growth by prioritizing speed over efficiency in an environment of uncertainty." And as the Agile Alliance points out: "It's really about thinking through how you can understand what's going on in the environment you're in today, identify what uncertainty you're facing, and figure out how you can adapt as you go along." Who wouldn't want that for their organization?

Chris Clearfield, author of the bestselling book *Meltdown: What Plane Crashes, Oil Spills, and Dumb Business Decisions Can Teach Us About How to Succeed at Work and at Home*, is an expert in dealing with—and thriving in—complex and often turbulent environments. After a career in high-speed trading, he now advises organizations and their leaders on how to set themselves up for success under those conditions. In between client calls and with him about to leave the house to rush to the airport, we caught up over a glitchy video call. Fast-talking yet softly spoken, he distilled the essence of agility: "Everybody wants to be agile; what's missed is—on a deep level—how much of a fundamental shift agile was in the way people operate, talk, discuss mistakes and problems, and ultimately work together."

In this context, we could benefit from going back to first principles (see what we did there?) and considering what agility truly is all about:

- Individuals and interactions over processes and tools
- Working products over comprehensive documentation
- Customer collaboration over contract negotiation
- Responding to change over following a plan

An agile approach consists of a set of core concepts, as pointed out by the Agile Foundation: personas and user stories specify our customers and encapsulate their jobs to be done; incremental and iterative development allows for quick iterations and incorporated learning along the way; and small teams, doing daily standup meetings and milestone retrospectives, allow for improved communication and further learning.

Joe Justice, a globally renowned leader in agile processes and former executive for agile practices at Tesla, Amazon, and the Bill & Melinda Gates Foundation, knows a thing or two about how to fill these principles with life.

"What matters is the pace of innovation" (Lex Clips 2021). These were the words Tesla's boss Elon Musk hammered into Justice's head when he joined the company to lead their agile manufacturing processes. Justice started by taking a lesson he learned from software mogul Bill Gates (another fanatically intense leader, just like Musk and Bezos) while working for Gates's foundation.

He sliced the work necessary to build a car into as many parallel executable tracks as possible. This first step increased Tesla's velocity by having multiple teams work side by side instead of the traditional sequential mode. The teams are no more than six people strong to keep them fast and nimble (in the following chapter on core and edge, we will dig deeper into the benefits of those small teams). By aggressively and relentlessly reducing the cost of change and incorporating quick feedback loops, the company managed to trim the time it takes to revise a car from months or years to three hours (Justice 2022). Tesla's approach to manufacturing a car is light years ahead of its competitors; the stock price does it justice.

The most successful organizations we encounter—the ones managing a dynamic, ever-changing landscape ripe with rapid state changes—are, universally, the ones successfully implementing these core principles across their organization. From tech giants like Amazon and Google to large, diversified enterprises like Grupo BRECA in Peru, all the way to founder-led businesses such as Axon and family-owned companies like Beiersdorf—by applying an agile approach to their respective businesses, they become and continue to be huge forces to reckon with. The respective implementation looks different from company to company and within a company from team to team—but they all found ways to focus on individuals and their interactions, release working products to their customers early, and iterate frequently.

Recalling advice given to her by London Business School's professor for organizational behavior Herminia Ibarra, Hannah Tucker likens the agile approach to "choosing an outfit in your wardrobe: you try something on, you wear it, you see how it fits and feels—and if it doesn't work out, you try something different the next day. We can so often be overwhelmed by what is happening and think we need to do something gigantic, whereas starting small and building on that is actually the way we can move forward."

Agility allows an organization to overcome its single most significant barrier to progress through process: when faced with challenging issues around disruption, people retreat to the familiar. They argue disruption can wait until tomorrow, as they have fires to put out today which require their attention right now. And, of course, "right now" never goes away. Maurice Conti puts it into stark terms: "This is one of the top failure modalities to innovation initiatives."

There always will be a fire to tend to, a problem to fix, or an issue arising. As an organization gets disrupted, those fires and issues will only multiply—resulting in us working harder and harder to try to make the current model of operating work. In many ways, it is insanity; as the famous quote, often misattributed to Albert Einstein, goes: "Insanity is doing the same thing over and over again and expecting different results." Agile approaches break this pattern by focusing attention on the customer's jobs to be done and breaking down tasks into small, iterative steps with feedback and learning loops built in.

Remember Rosini's paper clip company? Paper clip companies love making paper clips. They are good at making paper clips. And making paper clips fits beautifully into a detailed and carefully designed five-year plan. But even the paper clip market shifts and people don't use all that much paper anymore, as everything is now on their smartphones and laptops. Suddenly, our paper clip company finds itself in a world of hurt—and instead of trying to figure out how to adapt to the new world quickly, the paper clip company executives focus on cutting costs, developing new, shinier versions of paper clips—really anything to keep the status quo intact. We all know how this story ends. And no, it isn't going to be a Disney movie ending. The better approach would have been to lean heavily into agility, run lots and lots of small experiments, learn from them, and thus move toward the future.

In his blog post "Software Is Process," Austin Vernon summarizes this: "Agile methods are a reason why software-driven challengers can fell even the most competent incumbents. Digitizing a process requires the challengers to know a business in more detail than the incumbents, and the challengers use systems that thrive with poor starting knowledge" (2021).

Cecilia Tham, the cofounder of think tank Futurity Systems, summarizes the overall approach succinctly: "It's never a straight line. It's never linear. And every first step you take, you're going to learn something new, and you need to reincorporate and recalculate and recalibrate. In a dynamic, fast-changing world, you've got to focus on speed. People are hungry for the ability to operate dynamically—and frankly, it is also much more fun. And being able to do this in an agile format is the only way to go."

Returning to our marketing example above, lots can be learned from what e-commerce giant eBay did over twenty years ago. Instead of running large, centrally coordinated (and expensive) campaigns, eBay's marketing team perfected the art of creating thousands of small online campaigns, each with a slightly different message. These campaigns were launched for a few hundred dollars and pitted against each other. In the style of a knock-out competition, the campaigns which performed better received more resources—until they themselves were knocked out by better-performing ones. The constant question the team asked itself was: How can we test our hypothesis with the fewest resources in the shortest amount of time?

Let me end this chapter about agility with a disclaimer: in some moments, you will want to slow down and not rush, but contemplate. "If you apply agile to absolutely every-thing, such as problem-solving or considering what the real question to be asked is, you really do yourself a disservice," reflects George Constantinescu. "Some things require you to dwell on them; they just take time. You need to be judicious how you spend your time on the things delivering most ben-efit—as Einstein also allegedly said: 'If I had an hour to solve a problem, I'd spend fifty-five minutes thinking about the problem and five minutes thinking about solutions.'" Make those five minutes agile (as you only have five minutes, there is no time to lose).

And most of all: fight the urge to jump to a solution too quickly.

TL;DR

To implement agile principles across the organization, consider the following points:

- Don't reduce "agility/agile" only to the Agile Software Development principles and approach or a specific methodology, such as scrum.
- Consider how you can become more agile across the whole organization. The essential tenets of agile principles can be deployed across (nearly) all functions and have the potential to reap huge benefits: (1) Parallelization of your workstreams. (2) Small, nimble teams (ideally no more than six people). (3) Goal Alignment across all teams. (4) Relentless reduction of the cost of making changes. (5) Robust and quick feedback loops.
- Avoid retreating to the familiar and start with small, calculated steps.
- In all the agile excitement and frenzy, don't forget to regularly "slow down to go fast."

3.2.3

Key 3: Core and Edge

To be, or not to be, that is the question.

—WILLIAM SHAKESPEARE, HAMLET

New and old, sustaining and innovating, generating cash flow and investing in the future—companies often have a core and an edge.

Global consulting firm McKinsey gave the world a way to think about an organization's investment alongside the triptych of three distinct time horizons (see chapter "Faults"), ranging from the here and now to the much further out world of research and development (2009). More generally speaking, companies have a core (where the vast majority of their activities happen) and an edge. Author and consultant John Hagel III defines the edge by stating "generally speaking, edges are peripheral areas with high-growth potential." He further describes the edge in the context of a business as "early-stage business initiatives with high-growth potential, whether new market-oriented initiatives or new work practices" (Hagel et al. 2009).

Another helpful aspect to consider is the core typically represents low or at least significantly lower risk. In contrast, the edge is high risk, as you have oodles of historical data and experience with your core operations, but, by definition, none of this at the edge. The core has high visibility; the edge is a thick fog you must navigate. You make the most of your money and generate cash flow for the current fiscal period in the core (and have the vast majority of your resources tied to the core) and lose money on the edge.

Maurice Conti, in our discussion, maps this distinction to R&D—which, in his language, doesn't stand for "Research & Development" but "Risk & Determinism": "The core must be a deterministic organization. All is planned and then executed according to plan. Don't mess around or take big risks with the core. The edge is all about risk. Building a team that knows how to take effective risks and is comfortable doing so. If the risk organization fails, literally nothing happens to the deterministic side of the business. No one even notices. But if the risk-taking is a success, it could reinvent the business, be worth billions, and ensure the long-term survival of the company."

Businesses need to have activity and investments in both parts of the organization. Conceptually, this is distinct as night and day—alas, nearly every organization we know of struggles with this in their operations. Without a healthy core, the organization simply ceases to exist, and without smart investments on the edge (both capital and operational), the company doesn't have a future.

Contrast this with the setup of a startup: startup companies are small and nimble. As such, they lack a resource advantage over established companies; their main advantage is their ability to move fast. Secondly, they are tightly focused on building a new business without the need to defend an existing one; startups are all in on making the new business happen and work. And lastly, the person in charge of the organization, typically the founder, has complete control over every element of the experience every step of the way. These three factors make startups such formidable opponents to incumbents—even though they are vastly smaller and operate with significantly fewer resources.

Andy Billings reminds us that in this context innovation, disruption, and transformation are closely linked to creativity: "All of us need to be innovative, and that always gets sparked by creativity. But how do you turn creativity into profitability? How do you keep the passion, fire, and creativity alive and still have predictable earnings?" Tasked with operating at the intersection of creativity and profitability, Billings starts the journey with a simple definition: creativity is taking capital and turning it into ideas; profitability is taking ideas and turning them into capital. To be successful, you need both, but you can't innovate without creativity.

The dichotomy between the here and now on one side and what's next on the other manifests itself deep in the fundamentals of how a company is run. The core of any organization, especially if it is an incumbent organization, has solid systems and processes in place to ensure it is being run as effectively, efficiently, and optimized as possible. All metrics and key performance indicators (KPIs) are finely tuned toward running a tight ship, maximizing uniformity in its output while minimizing variation.

Decades of management theory, thinking, and practice have ensured companies are good, if not great, at this. Efficient markets have put further pressure on market participants to either sail or sink—and while they are at it, become excellent at sailing. An organization's core can be compared to an aircraft carrier, to stay in the nautical metaphor. Once set in motion, stopping is hard, and turning quickly is impossible.

Compare this to edge initiatives, typically exploratory in nature, offering exponential growth potential coupled with an equal amount of risk for failure. By their very definition, these initiatives are not at a stage where they are effective, efficient, or optimized for financial outcomes; on the contrary, edge initiatives are designed to increase an organization's learning and insights into new markets, products, services, customer segments, or technologies. Instead of being a giant aircraft carrier, they resemble a speedboat: nimble, fast, and highly maneuverable, but also very limited in their capacities.

Imagine a traditional car manufacturer exploring the "connected car"—the future vehicle sometimes described as "an iPhone on wheels." Leaders in this organization must manage two fundamentally different businesses at the same time. They need to be able to walk into one meeting, analyze the latest set of KPIs, and push their organization to squeeze any possible efficiency gains out of their existing car manufacturing processes—and then walk across the hallway into a meeting of their connected car team, forget any heuristic used in the previous meeting, and ask, "What have we learned today?" It might sound easy, but doing it in practice is remarkably hard.

And it is not only confined to your KPIs but runs deep in the structure of an organization. Rick Smith recalls when his company added a software-as-a-service business to its existing hardware sales and thus needed to bring in software salespeople, working alongside the company's existing traditional salespeople. "Our existing sales reps were bringing in $10–15 million a year; in this line of business, this meant a salary of $150,000 per year. Now we had to bring in different talent, people who knew how to sell software. And these people come from different backgrounds and have very different expectations toward their compensation; suddenly, we are talking $300,000 per year. And as this is a new business, we initially had zero sales. Well, people talk, and the existing business looks at me and asks, 'What the heck is going on? Why are we doing this?' We had a damn near civil war. It was super painful; the internal battles were actually harder than the customer battle. But you have to stand your ground and manage both sides of the business appropriately to its needs and unique setup."

Lisa Kay Solomon at Stanford's d.school likens this skill—which is incredibly hard to learn and sustain—to one's ability to be ambidextrous. Ambidexterity, the ability to use both the right and left hand equally well, is an apt metaphor for what is required of the leader of the future: the ability to manage the core and the edge of an organization at the same time. The concept first came into existence in the mid-nineties, when Michael Tushman together with Charles O'Reilly published a paper, defining organizational ambidexterity as "the ability to simultaneously pursue both incremental and discontinuous innovation … from hosting multiple contradictory structures, processes, and cultures within the same firm" (1996).

Andy Billings successfully fuses these two sides by spending time with the creatives in the company, explaining to them the necessity for profits to keep the proverbial lights on (and further fund their creative endeavors). Not surprisingly, Billings found even the most creative people on his team knew how to balance their budgets at home, and had mortgages to pay and money to save for their kids' college education. Yet, in the early days of this effort, Billings found himself talking to a group of creatives about spending thousands and thousands of dollars for graphical items that were only used in the backdrop of games; they didn't materially improve the gaming experience. Once the creatives started to consider their decisions' impact on the financial viability of the game they were creating, the same artists came to Billings and said: "We are not going to do this anymore. We'd rather spend the money on game characters; the elements which have a direct, measurable impact on our players' satisfaction."

The question becomes, how do you translate what Billings managed to do on the individual and team level to the whole organization? And how do you manage the often-inevitable tension emerging from the core and the edge rubbing against each other?

MANAGING THE TENSION

From "completely separate core and edge" to "deeply integrated core and edge"—much ink has been spilled in providing often somewhat dogmatic advice on how to manage the challenges which arise from managing, and managing well, the core and the edge.

In much of his work, John Hagel III points out the only way to handle the tension between both parts of an organization is the strict separation of both sides. Combined with a deliberate resource restriction of the edge ("starve the edge") to ensure the teams operating at the edge stay hungry, the edge develops largely independent of the core—and eventually, should the effort turn out to be successful, grows into the new core. Figuratively, the young will eat their old.

Contrast this with the advice given by Chris Yeh, who suggests organizations create a permeable membrane between the core and the edge by placing leaders who can straddle both hemispheres—in other words, who are ambidextrous—at the intersection between core and edge. Organizations failing to do so regularly invoke autoimmune system responses (see our chapter on the four horsemen).

Michael Arena, the author of *Adaptive Space: How GM and Other Companies are Positively Disrupting Themselves and Transforming into Agile Organizations*, recalls the moment when car manufacturer GM acquired autonomous driving startup Cruise (2018). To overcome the organization's autoimmune response, as well as a healthy dose of "not invented here" syndrome (where many at GM, as a leader in the automobile manufacturing space, believed GM could build their own autonomous vehicle tech without the need of an acquisition), CEO Mary Barra surprisingly tasked GM's chief engineer to run the newly acquired business.

Going from managing and being responsible for 25,000 people to running a nascent business unit of 300 people in the heart of Silicon Valley, far away from GM's headquarters, might seem strange. In Barra's view, it was not only the right but also the only thing to do; Cruise represents the company's future, and you can find someone else to run the established, well-oiled machinery representing the current business. For the core to not reject the edge, Barra required someone whom the people inside the organization were willing to listen to, whom they respected and trusted to lead the organization into the future. This overlapping space between core and edge is what Arena dubbed the adaptive space.

And lastly, you will find thought leaders calling for complete integration of core and edge inside the organizational umbrella, arguing innovation is everyone's job. Resources need to be shared extensively to leverage economies of scale and scope both for the traditional core and emerging edge initiatives.

We don't believe in dogma or a world neatly separated into black and white. And while we don't question the logic or success of the three approaches (and any permutations thereof), we have seen with clients globally the specific implementation should primarily be driven by who you are (as an organization), your culture, which market you are in, how innovation happens inside your market, and where you are regarding emerging state changes.

That being said, in our work and through our extensive interviews, we identified three essential elements of how to successfully set up your key business units—regardless of your organizational setup. Instead of providing dogmatic solutions, we formulate these elements as questions to ask of your organization rather than answers to be implemented blindly. Any specific structure or solution must be an expression of the respective insight from each element, combined with your organization's culture.

And it all starts, as usual, with your people.

HUNTERS, NOT FARMERS

When was the last time you saw a company launch a new billion-dollar initiative and reward the team behind it with a $25 million bonus? It hardly ever happens; instead, we give the team a golden watch. One of the most fundamental elements any organization must figure out—to be successful in their edge initiatives—is the answer to the question of how your company rewards risk-taking.

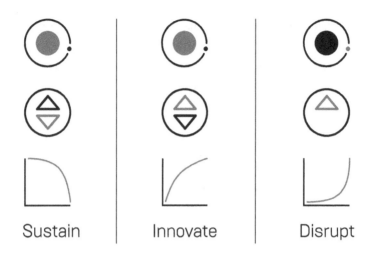

| Sustain | Innovate | Disrupt |

Three Spheres of Business

When looking at innovation across an organization, one can differentiate three distinct spheres. An organization's core engages in innovation initiatives—Clayton Christensen's idea of "sustaining innovation" (2022). We like to further differentiate the core activities by looking at the longer-term market potential: in markets showing a long-term decline (and eventual disappearance), companies typically play a game of defense. You innovate to sustain your current market share, squeeze out operational efficiencies, and often find yourself in a very stable, predictable cash-generating position. Accordingly, we refer to this position as one of "sustaining the core."

Meanwhile, within the core, you frequently find new opportunities which present growth potential—line extensions, new customer segments, new use cases, and up- and cross-selling. Companies play offense in these markets, driven by their core activities and resources. We commonly refer to this as "innovation from the core."

And lastly, as you spot state changes, you deploy edge initiatives aimed at playing a strong offensive game in an exponentially growing market. In these initiatives, "disruption" happens.

Following Southwest Airlines founder Herb Kelleher's famous insight "the business of business is people—yesterday, today, and forever" (HSMAmericas 2008), the question becomes: Who are the people operating at their best in each sphere? Do you have the right people, and are they in the right place to be successful?

To illustrate the point, let's map the prototypical person in each sphere to one of three archetypes: farmers, gatherers, and hunters.

FARMERS SUSTAIN THE CORE.

Farmers lovingly tend to the crops on the homestead. They spend their days caring for the seedlings, ensuring crops have all their nutrients and water, tending to the soil, and preventing bugs from getting to the crops. Their primary concern is to ensure the harvest is a full one and that they squeeze every last ounce of yield out of the land they have. After a long day, the farmer enjoys the fruit of their labor, sipping cold lemonade and watching the sun go down from their porch. When it's time for bed, they close the shutters, cuddle into their comfortable bed, and dream of ideal weather, no pests, and a rich harvest.

GATHERERS INNOVATE FROM THE CORE.

Gatherers enjoy their life outdoors. They get up with the first rays of the sun, grab their knapsack, and jump the fence of the homestead. The gatherer is on a mission to find fruit and honey, so they go off into the surrounding meadows, climb trees, shake ripe apples off their branches, pick cherries, and carefully approach the beehive, searching for honey. Gatherers love to be out in the wild, finding new and exciting things to eat and telling stories of their discoveries over the homestead's fire pit in the evening. As much as gatherers enjoy being outside, they do everything to be back before the sun sets; they know very well this is when the wild animals appear. And the comfort of their bed is undoubtedly something to be treasured.

HUNTERS ARE DISRUPTORS OPERATING AT THE EDGE.

Lastly, you have the crazy ones, the misfits, the rebels— the hunters. Hunters love the thrill of the hunt. Hunters are deeply curious and driven by a craving for adrenaline, adventure, and the wilderness, combined with an abnormally high tolerance for discomfort and suffering, so hunters prefer sleeping under the stars over any warm bed. Hunting the wooly mammoth, they risk their lives over and over again until they are successful—or die doing so. Equally driven by the experience itself, the knowledge should they be successful (the homestead has enough protein for a whole winter), and a desire to be celebrated as heroes upon their return, hunters trade high risk for high reward.

BUILDING THE FARMSTEAD

With those three archetypes, the question is: Do you have (enough) hunters in your organization? And if you do, are they deployed at the edge, where they belong? How do you compensate them, knowing hunters like to take outlandish risks but also expect sufficient compensation? How do you bring all three types together to form a tightly knit and successful tribe where they work with each other and not as soloists? And might you have farmers or gatherers working hunter jobs?

What we found over the years is a pattern repeating itself: even if you have hunters in your organization, have identified them, and deployed them at the edge (where they belong and want to be), nearly no reward systems are set up to align with the risks a hunter is taking. When was the last time you rewarded an executive and their team for building a new business, business unit, or product/service with a paycheck matching the return of said project for the organization? In simple terms, when was the last time you gave someone a $10 million bonus for building a $100 million business? Organizations don't tend to do this for numerous (good) reasons. Instead, we give our hunter the proverbial golden watch and see them leave for greener pastures.

Hunters leave incumbents in droves for startups for many reasons; one of the main ones is the misalignment of risk and reward. Remember: hunters risk their lives (in today's world, thankfully more likely their careers) to do the seemingly impossible; they (rightfully) expect to be compensated richly should they, against the odds, succeed. Combine this with the still predominant tendency to reward and promote people in organizations for obedience, conformity, and status, and you see why it is so incredibly hard for incumbents to hire, promote, and retain hunters.

Tom Chi, a founding member of Google X, likens the challenge of creating and running an edge project to rolling a die: we know any edge initiative has a relatively low chance of success. LinkedIn's founder and venture capital investor at Greylock, Reid Hoffman, puts this very directly: "The default outcome is probably failure or death" (2020). Contrast this with the context of large(r) organizations, which devote themselves to reducing the possibility of failure, and you can spot the misalignment. Now assume you take one of the high performers inside your company, give them a six-sided die, let them roll it, and tell them if it comes up with a six, the initiative succeeds and they get promoted. Any other result and the initiative fails, their career will stall, or they will get fired. How many people do you know who will play this game? The sad truth is this is precisely the deal we tend to offer the hunters inside our organizations. The good news is you have two ways to make this work: one, increase the reward, and two, empower the high performer to roll the dice more than once (by deploying key two—agile everywhere), which will significantly increase their chance of success.

A related issue arises when you deploy gatherers—or even worse, farmers—in positions typically staffed with hunters. This is often a result of the well-intended way promotions happen inside of organizations: we rightfully reward high performance, promote our people, and give them new challenges to grow into. On this well-trodden path, it is easy to forget most people have a somewhat fixed appetite for risk—not to be confused with Carol Dweck's seminal work on the fixed versus growth mindset (2007).

We know from the approach people take to their personal finances that an individual has a certain tolerance for risk. From those who invest most of their money in low-yield savings accounts to the ones who are playing the stock market, all the way to those who are using leveraged assets to buy futures, financial institutions have long understood their clients are different when it comes to their comfort with risk.

The same is true for an individual's appetite for risk-taking when it comes to their job and the work they do. Promoting a high-performing farmer who left their mark on the core of an organization to a hunter position on the edge is typically a recipe for disaster: not only is it highly likely the farmer won't perform in their new role, but they will also be stressed out and uncomfortable operating in a risk environment far outside their comfort zone.

To build on what Jim Collins wrote in his bestselling book *Good to Great: Why Some Companies Make the Leap ... and Others Don't* (2001), it is important to "get the right people on the bus"—but also make sure you put them into the right seats and create the appropriate reward structures for them.

As a fair warning: not everyone in your organization will be along for the ride, regardless of whether they are farmers, gatherers, or hunters. As David Bray, Principal at LeadDo-Adapt Ventures, shared from his experience both in private sector companies and large-scale governmental organizations, "there are always laggards—the 15 percent of people

I don't (and can't) focus on, as they are never coming along for the ride."

Embrace having hunters around. Like children, they can be hard work but are so much fun to hang out with. And they will make your company better.

SMALL TEAMS GENERATE NEW PROBLEMS TO SOLVE

Large teams solve problems, and small teams generate new problems to solve. Dashun Wang, associate professor of management and organizations at the Kellogg School of Management, and his colleagues analyzed over sixty-five million scientific papers, patents, and software products created between 1954 and 2014 to study the implications of team size on productivity (Brett & Wang 2020). Wang used an established measure of disruption to assess how much a given work destabilizes its field by creating new directions of inquiry versus building on existing ideas and designs to address existing problems. Their findings are summarized in the opening statement of this paragraph, which has important implications on how edge projects should be set up.

"Starve the edge." This is John Hagel III summarizing the approach in his report on "Unleashing motivation for transformation" (2022). Hagel goes on to point out "our natural instinct is to pour as much money as we can into promising edge initiatives to ensure their success. It is a temptation we ought to resist, as the more money an organization diverts into edge initiatives, before any tangible impact is delivered, the more vulnerable those projects will be to the immune system response to retrieve that money."

And it is not only the immune system response making small teams superior in the context of edge initiatives. "Communication pathways" is a fancy way of describing the number of connections between team members. Three people have three pathways. Add one person to the team, and the pathway count goes up to six. For a six-person team to be fully in sync, fifteen links are still manageable but already add some overhead. Create a group of ten, and you drown in forty-five communication pathways.

Add to this the various other challenges of large groups, starting with process losses—where challenges with the coordination of information and motivation accumulate and interact with each other exponentially, resulting in a reduction of a team's productivity—compounded by the common knowledge effect, where team members talk about what everyone already knows, rather than the unique information possessed by just one member of the group. Layering in the social effects of large(r) teams, including relational loss (when team members believe they have little support from other team members), loss of social cohesion (our feeling of belonging, connection, and unity), social loafing (conforming to a group's social norms), and usually only very few team members doing the lion's share of talking in meetings, and it becomes apparent large teams, as necessary as they are for scaled-up core activities, are poisonous for edge initiatives.

Whatever the specific team size of your edge initiatives is, keep them as small as possible and add new team members cautiously. By doing so you not only reap the benefits outlined before, but also create hyper, cross-functional teams (out of necessity) with high levels of spatial awareness, resulting in better coordination across the organization.

During my time at eBay Germany in 2001/2002, when it generated half as much as the total revenue of the mothership in the US in a significantly smaller geography, we ran the whole company with fewer than 150 people. We followed a mantra of "hiring behind the curve"—only adding new members to the team when we knew for sure we needed them and the work couldn't be done by other team members anymore. In other words, we were successful at starving the edge.

Drawing on an image from the wondrous world of botany, Gustav Strömfeld, the former lead for the blockchain portfolio and innovation accelerator at the World Food Program, compares this approach to the way you grow orchids—a notoriously hard-to-grow-at-home flower (technically a weed, but we won't be splitting hairs over this): you deliberately do not water an orchid all that much, as the orchid, when slightly dehydrated, will move its energy from growing yet another leaf into growing a stem which results in a beautiful flower.

If starvation isn't your jam, Amazon's founder Jeff Bezos famously coined the term "two-pizza team rule." No team should be larger than what you can comfortably feed with two large pizzas—same idea, same result, different metaphor.

CONTROL OVER THE EXPERIENCE

You have set up your edge initiative, staffed it with hunters, and followed the two-pizza rule. The last step in empowering your edge team is to give them control over the experience, a seemingly simple and benign step, yet one which can significantly impact your ability to innovate and develop transformational products or services fit for an emerging state change.

Often referred to as "freedom within a framework" or "freedom within a system," companies tend to set clear guardrails regarding how a new product or service can look, feel, perform, and be produced, marketed, and sold. The guardrails ensure the integrity and safety of the overarching brand, as well as consistency and familiarity across the brand. All of these work well and provide many benefits for situations that call for, in Clayton Christensen's vernacular, "sustaining innovation." Think about the humble laundry detergent. It exists in many forms, from the classic washing powder (solid soap before that) to the newer tabs, pods, and liquids. One thing stays the same: it is always, unmistakably, laundry detergent.

This works great—until you encounter a state change and most, if not all, the rules are thrown out the window. Now the framework or system becomes a hindrance and liability which new entrants don't have to contend with as they don't have to battle with legacy.

When operating at the edge, teams need to have complete control over the experience to focus on the customer's jobs to be done and to create without limitations.

SodaStream, the company producing their namesake home carbonation device since 1903, making sparkling water in the comfort of one's home with the press of a button, was acquired by beverage and snack giant PepsiCo in 2018. Despite a strong user base across Europe (20 percent of households in Sweden owned a SodaStream machine in 2010) (Zalik 2010), the company had a hard time establishing itself in the US market primarily due to US consumers not drinking much sparkling water. The challenge in the US market was compounded by the fact that to exchange the empty carbon dioxide cylinder, consumers had to find a local supermarket—such as Target, which carried SodaStream cylinders—hand in their empty cylinders, and exchange them for a refilled one. This hassle proved just too much for many consumers.

Under the leadership of PepsiCo's visionary CEO Ramon Laguarta and after observing a state change where consumers now shop for food-related items online, the SodaStream team hatched a plan to create a seamless direct-to-consumer experience to exchange their empty CO_2 cylinders for full ones. Consumers would go on SodaStream's website, order a full CO_2 cylinder, and use the empty packaging from the shipment they received to send their empty one back.

Laguarta gave this edge initiative complete control over the experience. Instead of requiring the team to work with the established IT infrastructure and vendors of PepsiCo, none of which was built for a direct-to-consumer experience, the team was free to operate like a startup. As every good startup does, the team first analyzed which software infrastructure was being used by other players in the direct-to-consumer space—no need to reinvent the wheel. Quickly, it became clear Canadian e-commerce software vendor Shopify was the predominant choice for most direct-to-consumer startups. Following these startups' footsteps, the SodaStream team built their online store using Shopify's software-as-a-service offering, paying only $2,000 per month and being up and running within weeks. One can only speculate what the upfront budget and running costs for a typical installation on PepsiCo's existing IT infrastructure would have been. Our estimate goes into the millions, and project lead times are measured in months and years, not weeks.

The most common, and usually hugely overestimated, objection toward giving edge initiatives control over the experience is reputational brand damage—a fear commonly overblown as edge efforts, by definition, are small, can be run under new brands, and—if communicated right—enjoy a lot of leeway from customers if they are told clearly what to expect. Google famously does this by slapping a "beta" label on most of their experimental initiatives.

Let go of your fear and lean into a little bit of messiness. The rewards will be rich. Not taking action or crippling an effort from the get-go are by far the worse options.

MANAGING THE TENSION

Speed *versus* quality—or is it speed *and* quality? Borrowing from Barry Johnson's 1992 bestseller, *Polarity Management: Identifying and Managing Unsolvable Problems*, the dichotomy of core and edge in a business can be seen as a polarity. Johnson defined a polarity as a pair of interdependent positive concepts working together for sustainable and optimal effectiveness. Leaders frequently have a positive view of one side of a polarity and a negative view of the other, or at least are biased toward one side. One side is privileged, and the other discounted, devalued, judged, or ignored.

The critical thing to understand about polarities is they are not problems to be solved, but rather dynamic tensions to be managed. Managing the tension between the core and edge requires ambidextrous leaders, putting (and keeping) the right people in the right positions, staying agile, quick, and nimble by setting up small, usually independent teams, and giving these teams the freedom to do what they need to do.

Next, let's explore what exemplifies a leader in this new world.

TL;DR

To successfully manage the tension between the core and the edge of your organization, consider the following points:

- Make sure you have the right people on the bus and have them in the right seats—especially your "hunters" (the disruptors).
- Create small, nimble teams for your edge initiatives by following Amazon's two-pizza rule.
- Empower your edge teams by giving them complete control over the experience.
- Connect the edge to the core by appointing people who are skilled at speaking to and influencing both sides.

Key 4: Leadership

Always do right. This will gratify some people and astonish the rest.

—MARK TWAIN

An endless number of articles, books, podcasts, workshops, and keynotes have dealt with the topic of leadership. Not surprisingly, no transformation can ever happen due to process and structure alone. Returning to Herb Kelleher's quote about businesses being about people, our behavior (i.e., leadership) becomes the focal point of change.

In our interviews and client work, my team at be radical and I identified five key leadership behaviors or skills present in all the leaders we worked with. They stand in addition to the leadership traits commonly discussed as the skills and behaviors necessary for future leaders, from empathy to agility, adaptability, and servant leadership.

1—COMMIT

How do leaders successfully move their organization from one state to the next? Maurice Conti, when asked this question, likes to tell a story:

Let me take you to the Wild West. A group of executives went and watched a classic cowboy movie. Picture Clint Eastwood riding into the sunset after having righted everything wrong with the world, the Colt in his holster still smoking. The moment the lights come back on in the cinema, our executives—empty popcorn bags still in their hands—look at each other and grin: "Wow, what a story. We need to think more like cowboys at our company!" And so, they head back to the office, their walk already a little broader and squarer (you know—from riding their imaginary horses across the Utah desert all day) and decide to bring in some cowboys to do "cowboy stuff" at the company. The excitement is palpable and genuine; the company will be so much better with some cowboys in their midst (by the way, these are the hunters of the previous chapter). The executives are truly enthusiastic about the innovative and risk-taking culture the cowboys (and cowgirls) will bring to the business.

A week into the endeavor, HR gathers up the cowboys and tells them: "We love, love, love what you are doing. Amazing stuff. But … there's just one thing. Your horses are pooping all over the office, and it's starting to smell a bit. Some of our other employees have started to complain. Honestly—it's a bit of a mess. Could we get rid of the horses and just use cars instead?"

The cowboys consider the request. Cars are safer and faster. Seems like they could still get their work done. Maybe they'll get some Ford F-150s. It's not such a big compromise …

A couple weeks later, the horses are gone, the cowboys are driving around in their new trucks, and the executives keep talking about how much the cowboys are changing the company's whole culture, how awesome it is to have them here, and how valuable they are.

At the end of their first month inside the corporation, the cowboys get another visit from HR. The company's chief people officer herself gushes how much they love the cowboys, how fantastic it is they are with the company—but ... the loaded revolvers are an issue. There are legal problems, other employees don't feel safe, and it's not a great fit for the company's brand. "Do you think maybe we could lose the guns? Would toy guns be okay?"

Again, the cowboys contemplate. This compromise to the way they do their work is big. The guns protect them from the very real risks they face. It's fundamentally part of who they are. But they love their jobs and are excited about their mission, so they agree. Somehow, they'll figure it out.

This keeps happening. Little by little and week by week, the things which make the cowboys "cowboys" keep getting chipped away. And then, six months later, you end up with a bunch of old, white guys in suits wearing big cowboy hats ... and that's just ridiculous.

As Jean-Paul Sartre once said, "Commitment is an act, not a word."

Commitment (and thus committing) in the context of an organization is deeply tied to how you think about and structure your incentives. George Constantinescu explains: "The world revolves around incentives; create the right incentive structures for people to have them do what we want them to do. Frequently, we have incentives doing the opposite, which prevent them from doing the right thing—even though they want to do the right thing. Take the whole incentive system rewarding the 'ready-made solution,' the quick fix. It feels good at the moment, but down the road, it leads to all kinds of unintended consequences and a lack of benefits. All of this is well intended: the governance structures, the gate-keeping processes, and the validation steps. All of those can (and are) being misused by using them as a line of defense instead of an enabler of opportunities. It makes successful companies retrench into optimization and protect the status quo."

Any innovation and thus transformation project requires its leaders to truly commit—not pay lip service to the often messy, uncomfortable changes necessary, but to be genuinely committed to the setup, process, and outcome. But committing—especially to a journey following an as-yet unknown path to a radically different destination—can be, and often is, scary. And it is not just us, but also our colleagues and subordinates.

2—COMMUNICATE

Everybody hates change—especially when it's being done *to* them. It is unsettling, uncomfortable, and often outright scary. Unless people both see a (much) better future for themselves and feel the burning urge to change, they won't change. They might say they will, but they won't. For change to happen, you need to provide both a compelling picture of the future—we like Jim Collins' acronym BHAG (2001): Big

Hairy Audacious Goals—and a solid response to the question of "Why should I change in the first place?"

Kyle Nel, former executive director for DIY retail giant Lowe's Innovation Labs, is a master of transformation. Nel stresses the need for a strategic narrative to drive change: "You have to have a real narrative with characters, conflict, and a narrative arc of where you are today and where you will be in the future. This is where we are going, and here is how we get there—the actual steps, the pathway, and how we break the bottlenecks in our organization on the way."

John F. Kennedy didn't tell the nation recent scientific and technological developments made it viable to create a cylindrical projectile that could be propelled to a great height or distance by the combustion of its contents, but instead created a spellbinding strategic narrative in his rousing speech on September 12, 1962, in Rice Stadium, Houston, Texas:

We choose to go to the moon. We choose to go to the moon in this decade and do the other things, not because they are easy, but because they are hard, because that goal will serve to organize and measure the best of our energies and skills, because that challenge is one that we are willing to accept, one we are unwilling to postpone, and one which we intend to win, and the others, too.

Nel contrasts this with the typical response to his inquiry: "I always ask leaders, what is your strategic narrative? And I explain very briefly what it is, and they'll usually give me some stupid strategy nonsense in a two-by-two grid. That's not a narrative; people don't get excited about a two-by-two grid."

Humans are hardwired for stories; we have conveyed information this way since time immemorial. From our forefathers sitting around the fire pit to JFK's famous moon speech, our brains and hearts react to well-crafted stories. Every single person we interviewed for our research reiterated the necessity of a compelling story. As Lisa Cron, author of the wonderful book *Wired for Story*, states: "Story evolved as a way to explore our minds and the minds of others, as a sort of dress rehearsal for the future" (2012).

One year before the end of World War II, Fritz Heider and Marianne Simmel conducted a landmark study (1944). Participants were shown a ninety-second cartoon animation depicting moving symbols—a box, two triangles, and a circle. When asked what the participants saw, most described the shapes as characters with recognizable emotions. Over the last six decades, the study has been replicated countless times, always with the same result: instead of seeing geometric shapes and symbols moving randomly across the screen, we see human interactions, household conflict, family drama, or love stories evolve. We seek and make meaning where none necessarily exists; we make sense of the world through story.

My colleague Jeffrey Rogers points out humans' desire for stories not only represents an opportunity for us to connect deeply through storytelling but also serves as an important reminder that everything we do will be understood in the context of stories—either the stories we tell or the stories told about us if we're not actively shaping and sharing the narrative.

Rogers shares four key elements necessary to craft your new narrative: your story must speak from your purpose, share your preferred future, include your audience, and show how they share the journey. Integrate those four building blocks into your strategic narrative, and you are well on your way. And forget the two-by-two matrix.

3—UNKNOW

If Silicon Valley is known for anything, it is its ability to start fresh. San Francisco-based software maker Autodesk is a pioneer in building creative tools for architecture, engineering, construction, manufacturing, media, education, and the entertainment industry. Before joining Telefónica, Maurice Conti was Autodesk's director for applied research and innovation.

One day, three weeks into his job and reporting directly to the chief technology officer, Conti found himself chatting with his boss. Conti describes his former boss as a "very, very smart guy—you need to pay attention when you're having a conversation with him just to keep up."

When asked what Conti should focus on in his new role, the CTO responded, "What I need you to do is go and look into our blind spots."

Conti was relieved. It was in line with what he imagined his job ought to be. Upon further thought, Conti blurted out: "So, by definition, you can't tell me where to go look?"

His boss nodded and said, "Exactly. I don't know. I can be a thought partner to help you once you find something, but I don't know where you ought to go look; that's the reason we hired you."

Saying these words—admitting you don't have the answer—takes courage. It goes against every learned behavior that made us successful in the first place. You received your grade A in school for providing the correct answer when the teacher asked a question. You got your college degree for knowing the answer to a problem. Furthermore, you got promoted for being the one who had the answer. Yet, in today's complex and uncertain world, as author Warren Berger points out in his book *A More Beautiful Question* (2014), the value of a discreet answer diminishes, and the value of a good question increases.

Leaders need to unknow—or unlearn—many of their deeply ingrained and tightly held beliefs and insights. You need to be able to send your team into the unknown on a near-impossible mission, where you won't be able to provide them with answers. The best you can do is provide direction, act as a sounding board for their ideas, and shield them from the autoimmune response an organization often wields against anything new and unknown. The destination is unknown.

The skill desperately needed in the future is a leader's ability to ask better questions, questions beginning with "Why?" or "What if?" or "How might we?" Stanford University professor Tina Seelig runs a workshop on "framestorming" instead of the typical brainstorming. In a framestorming session, the goal is to generate more and better questions—not seek answers. Seelig likes to remind her students "questions are the frames into which the answers fall." When we generate questions rather than solutions, we dig deep into a problem and challenge assumptions. The process permits people to ask fundamental questions that often don't get asked—not just "How can we do it better?" but also "Why are we doing this in the first place?"

To run your own question generation session, start with identifying the "question focus," which is easiest done in the form of a provocative statement (e.g., "A quarter of our customers are unhappy with our delivery times"). Once you identify the question focus, split the team into groups of four to six people and have them generate as many questions as they possibly can come up with in ten minutes. After reviewing and improving the generated questions, you prioritize them and decide on the next steps.

The pivotal question for the leader of the future is: How do you lead into and in the unknown? Not knowing the answer is a troubling feeling—but one we need to get comfortable with. Ask yourself how comfortable you are with being uncomfortable.

4—INVERT

Ever since the days of the Roman army, we have tended to borrow our organizations' leadership and organizational design from how the military structures itself. From Taylor's insights on work specialization and Fayol's chain of command to Weber's bureaucracy, we design our systems to maximize productivity and efficiency. Probably the most visible manifestation of these approaches is the organizational chart—neatly drawn boxes connected by lines and a clear chain of command from top to bottom.

Whether this ever actually worked is debatable, as the people at the bottom of the organizational chart commonly trample over those neatly drawn boxes and lines in their effort to get their job done—a behavior we commonly diagnose as a failure mode of the people walking over those geometric shapes rather than a problem with our organizational setup.

Organizational charts and their top-down structure of command and control require a stable and predictable environment. One where we can project years, sometimes decades, into the future with a high degree of certainty and where the dominant question is one of efficiency, effectiveness, and optimization. These organizations are managed linearly—moving from A to B in a straight line, commonly expressed through the "five-year plan." Organizations gather information—often through an involved strategy process—develop their strategic plan based on this information, and then go about executing it until it is time for the next plan.

Today's environment is a highly interconnected and interdependent system with a significant degree of volatility, uncertainty, complexity, and ambiguity—a world commonly referred to by the acronym "VUCA." (Bennis 1986) The environment we operate in changes so frequently and so dramatically that by the time a classic strategy process is completed, the information said plan is based on has already changed, rendering the plan obsolete.

Dee Hock, founder and former CEO of the Visa credit card association, described in a dinner speech at the famous Santa Fe Institute his approach to running Visa, for a long time the world's largest card payment organization, as a system combining both chaos and order, coining the term "chaordic" (1999). By acknowledging our operating environments exhibit high degrees of "VUCA" and combining it with an organization's need for (some) order, Hock created Visa as a highly decentralized organization—in turn creating an organizational management blueprint which today has been adopted by leading disruptors such as Amazon, Google, and the company I had the fortune of working with, Mozilla.

Have you ever seen a murmuration of starlings do their intricate, mesmerizing dance in midair? It is a sight to behold and an apt metaphor for how we ought to run our businesses, particularly our edge initiatives. Every starling, at any given time, takes in and processes three key components.

The first component is the overall direction of their migratory path. Each individual bird knows its "North Star"—the general direction and destination of its migratory route. Your North Star provides clarity. It answers the simple yet powerful question: "Are we clear on where we are going?"

The second factor is the environment—the wind, sources of lift, air pressure, humidity, etc. In our world, this equates to every person on our team permanently orienting themselves on the actions of their fellow teammates, scanning what is going on in the market, new developments in the core and adjacent areas of the business, and shifts in customer expectation and behavior. The organization becomes a sensing one, where every person on the team not only executes but also seeks out and processes new information.

The final component, as was pointed out in a scientific paper published in the journal *Proceedings of the National Academy of Sciences* by Sara Brin Rosenthal et al., is "the rapid transmission of local behavioral response to neighbors" (2015). The best teams operate in the same way. Every member relays newfound insights back to the broader organization—not in a highly centralized way (the dreaded "intranet") but in practical, actionable insights relayed to the people on the team who can take action on the new findings. By relying on these three factors, starlings move—leaderless, highly effective, and efficient—through the air while minimizing energy expenditure. Starlings don't have (or need) organizational charts.

Drawing inspiration from biology, the most innovative, disruptive, and transformative businesses and edge initiatives operate with the same core principles. Instead of aiming to get the strategy right and then embark on a linear path, executing a preset strategy, their leaders focus on getting the direction right, setting the North Star for the organization or initiative and focusing on a first-principle-derived description of where we want to be in the future. Conveying the organization's direction through a strong and compelling strategic narrative, these leaders then enable and empower their teams to act largely autonomously—where each individual team member, at any given moment, considers both the environment and insights gained from their peers to make quick, iterative decisions. This results in a pattern that isn't a straight line but rather something which Corey Ford, CEO of media-focused startup accelerator Matter, described as "the drunken walk of the entrepreneur/intrapreneur."

The old world was top-down. Commands, barked by the C-suite, were communicated through the ranks with an expectation of somewhat mindless execution. In the new, current, and future world, the leaders of a company task themselves with setting the direction and creating the environment for their teams to flourish. They understand those with the most profound, fundamental, first-principles-based understanding of the customer and what is going on in the market are at the bottom of a traditional org chart. These leaders make use of this information by letting it flow freely, unencumbered, and unfiltered to the top—informing and shaping the way the company moves, step by step, on its journey.

Hock incorporated these nature-inspired design principles into how he built Visa and formed a collective, cocreated organization run by its tens of thousands of member banks globally. In the process, he codified his insights into management and organizational theory and practice, calling them chaordic systems.

Firefox creator Mozilla modeled itself on Hock's pioneering approach. In turn, Mozilla created one of the most significant open-source projects globally with, in its heyday, 500 million users all around the world, powered by millions of lines of software code and available in more than sixty languages—all cocreated by a global army of volunteer coders, hackers, and marketers, with enthusiasts and fewer than 200 people (back in 2009 when I was at Mozilla) employed by Mozilla itself. The organization might be unique in its specific approach and history, yet the key pillars on which it was built are not unique and are those which you find at the center of the very best organizations in the world.

Four essential components are the nucleus of companies such as Amazon and Google, countless unicorn startups (companies with a valuation of $1 billion and above), the very best edge initiatives in incumbent companies, and—of course—Visa (at the time):

- Strong agreement on the core principles (as Hock pointed out, this is where you want to spend a disproportionate amount of time and energy, as it sets up the system for dynamic but structured tension between cooperation and competition)
- Distribution of the decision making to the edges of the organization
- Giving authority to the edges to make their own decisions
- Fostering the free flow of information across the whole organization in any direction

Taken together, these principles form the basis for the success of companies such as Google or Amazon. Google's and Amazon's flat hierarchies, small teams (the two-pizza rule at Amazon), willingness and ability to experiment (the famous 20 percent projects, where Google allows any employee to spend 20 percent of their time to work on projects which are unrelated to their primary job), open sharing of information on company intranets, and informal ways of teams and groups working together, collaborating, and sharing—these all lead to an inverted organizational structure, resembling a murmuration of starlings on their way south rather than an army marching into the sunset.

5—PERSIST

Silicon Valley lore says, "Every overnight success was five to ten years in the making." What seems like companies and their services or products coming out of nowhere and taking over the world are usually not toddlers but, more often than not, middle schoolers. Take a look at many of the most iconic startups (which have become successful grown-ups). You see the pattern: Airbnb, founded in the fall of 2007, announced precisely five years later it served nine million guests since launch—and thus moved out of its niche and established itself as a serious competitor in the hospitality space. Ride-sharing company Uber was founded about a year after Airbnb, in the winter of 2008. After five years of feverish work, Uber announced their one-hundredth city where you could hail one of their cars using the Uber app—the moment Uber established itself as a truly relevant player in the market.

And it is not just the startups, as Gisbert Rühl at German steel distribution giant Klöckner & Co points out: "Our digital transformation, even though it was hailed as an overnight success, was not something we could do overnight. When we started in 2014, I was convinced it needed time—although I didn't expect it to take the six years it took in the end. It took definitely longer than I expected." (We'll hear more of this story in the next chapter.)

We're back to Ernest Hemingway's idea of "gradually, then suddenly" (1954). This is an idea often used to describe the exponential nature of change—be it brought about by technology (e.g., the smartphone, as we saw earlier), but also the very nature of edge initiatives (with startups operating on the edge by their very definition).

Keeping this in mind when embarking on your journey to the edge is essential, as the journey will be long and arduous. German media company Axel Springer, one of the few shining examples of an incumbent transitioning from a print business to a predominantly digital one, took twenty years for this journey—a journey which, as Axel Springer's leadership gladly admits, isn't over yet (and might never be completed). A journey requiring us to persist—as this necessity for persistence, patience, and longevity of edge initiatives flies into the face of how most modern-day firms are organized.

According to an Equilar study from 2017, the median tenure for a Fortune 500 CEO was five years—and declining rapidly (in 2013, the median tenure was a full year longer)—resulting in most CEOs at large corporations not seeing their edge initiatives through to the end (Marcec 2018). Even worse, companies frequently move their high-potential leaders from one area of responsibility to another within the organization.

This, of course, happens for good reasons: you want to develop and groom emerging talent inside your company, and the best way to do this is to expose them to as many novel situations, inputs, and challenges as possible. But it flies in the face of the reality of edge initiatives—as they simply need more time to mature than the tenure of the average leader on the project tends to have. The result? Projects running out of steam, loss of institutional knowledge, direction, and vision, and leadership "whiplash". The norm for a new leader coming into an existing project is typically to "leave their mark" by redefining the vision, changing the direction, as well as operating procedures (and sometimes people working on the project).

Combining these challenges with the sometimes-held view that transformation is a journey with a beginning and an end, a "from-to" proposition rather than a continuous process, where it is not about "getting through" transformation but, rather, "living in" transformation, it becomes apparent how the deck can be stacked against an organization.

Now might be a perfect moment to reflect on your journey and mull over the question, "What will you be doing five years from today?"

Leadership, not surprisingly, is at the core of every transformation. It goes hand in hand with organizational design. Leading yourself is not enough; you need to create the structures to enable and empower others to lead. The good news is good leadership is neither complicated nor complex. It simply requires commitment and hard, ongoing work—on yourself and your organization.

TL;DR

To lead into and in the unknown, consider the following points:

- Commit to the outcomes of your edge initiatives, not just the process.
- Communicate through storytelling by speaking from your purpose, sharing your preferred future, including your audience, and showing them how they share the journey.
- Become comfortable and proficient in leading into the unknown by overcoming the urge to "know the answer" and instead lean into asking better questions.
- Invert existing organizational structures by providing directions instead of strategy, allowing for continuous course corrections along the way, and empowering your frontline workers to act as a sensory network.
- Create organizational structures, compensation, career pathways, and incentives for your people to persist through the transformational journey. Consider the interdependence of your leaders—the way they work together across levels and geographies. Your leaders need to operate independently, yet in service of the whole.

3.2.5

Key 5: Re/Upskilling

We live in the world our questions create.

—*DAVID COOPERRIDER*

Every transformation, every state change, will alter the game you play. Today you might be playing tennis—a game performed on a court, using a racket and balls, aiming to smash the ball over a net to ensure your opponent can't return the ball to you. Tomorrow, you might find yourself on a cricket field—holding a bat in your hand loosely resembling the familiar tennis racket. It is still a game where you smash a ball with the aim of your opponent not being able to catch it. Alas, it not only looks and feels different, but is also played by an entirely different set of rules. Further, it requires not only using other equipment, playing on foreign turf, and learning a different gameplay; you also need to establish new movement patterns and have your muscles challenged in very different ways.

Imagine moving from renting out VHS videotapes to local customers in a store to streaming video content straight to people's televisions, transitioning from selling rolls of film to creating an app to apply creative filters to a digitally captured photo, or shifting from selling copies of your software to renting out software in a software-as-a-service model. These are all state changes and all new games to master (although they often have some resemblance to what came before).

Organizations, by and large, know re- and upskilling their workforce is essential. Yet, the typical efforts resemble something like this: management tasks HR with ensuring the organization's workforce is ready for the company's digital transformation. With the best intentions, HR seeks learning opportunities and programs—one set of programs for upper and middle management and then a more scalable, price-efficient solution for the rest of the company.

As a result, upper management gets shipped off to Silicon Valley for a week-long "immersion tour," where the company visits startups and venture capital firms and generally immerses itself in the culture of the fifty miles between San Francisco and San Jose. Meanwhile, HR blissfully signs an agreement with one of the many online learning providers to deliver learning for the rest of the company—believing (and hoping) employees embark on a "choose your own adventure" journey using these online learning platforms and emerge with new skills and a refreshed mindset. The belief (and hope) is both insights are gained, and cultural shifts are achieved; these, in turn, permeate out from those who attended the trip to the rank and file upon return from sunny California.

Of course, none of this ever works.

The reality is upper management had a great time on their trip to Silicon Valley, experienced a fair (and sometimes extreme) amount of culture shock, didn't learn anything as all their interactions were only skin deep and out of context, and ended up buying a bunch of Google T-shirts at the Google campus store. Meanwhile, the rank and file either entirely ignore their invitation to "learn" as it would require time they don't have, or they pick courses that pique their interest (and might not be aligned to their work at all) only to abandon them after the first session, as the content felt irrelevant, the learning modality didn't work out, the time commitment was too high, or the course was poorly produced.

Bill Pasmore—professor of practice of social organizational psychology at Teachers College, Columbia University—recalls an episode from his work at the Center for Creative Leadership where one of the board members took an executive team from an incumbent organization on a Silicon Valley immersion trip. What the executives saw on the trip was so overwhelming—so far out of their comfort and knowledge zone—it scared them into inaction: "It scared them so much they had no ability to cope with what they were seeing and no skills or ability to plot a course toward the future. So, they just went back to what they knew, hanging on and hoping they can get by with making do with what they're currently doing and leave the real adaptation to disruption."

Yet, as Pasmore points out, the conundrum of effective learning is this: "We know leaders don't learn primarily by reading books or watching YouTube videos (side note: it is not lost on us that you are reading a book right this moment). Even though we would like to think it's the case—but actually, what we know about adult learning is 70 percent of it happens through experience."

Today's learning is based chiefly on patterns we draw from our school or educational experiences, which we transplant into the workplace. As Lars Hyland, chief learning officer at Totara Learning, points out: "When you look at the learning process itself, it's multimodal; we need to be stimulated. We need focused, allocated time for learning; we need time to reflect on what we have learned and practiced—and practice has to happen in our work context to be effective."

We need to relearn to learn—for ourselves and our people.

RESKILLING AT WORK

Who says you can't transform a steel company into a digital powerhouse? In 1906, merchant Peter Klöckner set up his namesake company Klöckner & Co (commonly abbreviated as KlöCo) as a trading company in Duisburg, Germany. The company soon became one of the largest German steel distributors and today ranks among Germany's 200 largest companies.

I first met Gisbert Rühl, KlöCo's CEO from 2009 until mid-2021, by way of introduction through a mutual friend at a small nondescript café in Cupertino, right in the heart of Silicon Valley. In close proximity to the Apple campus, the café is frequented by Apple's employees seeking a quiet spot away from the prying eyes of the corporate mothership to talk about career opportunities outside of Apple or ideas for a startup. In the midst of hushed conversations, with the café's iconic red velvet latte in hand, Rühl shook my hand and introduced himself with the words, "Hi, I am Gisbert."

Here is a fifty-six-year-old CEO of a traditional German steel company introducing himself by his first name, disregarding the long-established German protocol which dictates one uses the last name when addressing another in a business setting. It was the appropriate beginning of a fascinating conversation.

Under his leadership, KlöCo launched a comprehensive digital transformation journey, spotting the signs of massive state changes happening in the steel industry. Rühl's team started with the complete digitization of KlöCo's supply chain. Far away from KlöCo's headquarters in the heart of Germany's traditional steel region, kloeckner.i—the group's center of competence for digitization—was placed in hip and trendy Berlin, the heart of Germany's startup scene. Sensing KlöCo's customers experienced significant friction in the fragmented market for steel products and operating on first principles and a profound understanding of its customers' jobs to be done, Rühl set out to create XOM Materials—a marketplace for the whole steel industry. In 2018, the company launched as an independent entity, inviting KlöCo's direct competitors onto the platform, serving clients industry wide—in many ways, the ultimate edge project.

Over multiple rounds of red velvet lattes and thus sufficiently caffeinated, Rühl walked me through the steps he took to transform a traditional steel company into a digital powerhouse and leader in its industry. Rühl's roadmap keyed on all four insights we've discussed in the earlier sections of this chapter—to then add an emphasis on key number five: the necessity to be deliberate about re- and upskilling your workforce.

To increase the "digital IQ" of the company, Rühl made the upskilling effort part of the management team's responsibility—starting with clearly defining which skills, knowledge, and mindset would be needed for KlöCo's workforce to be competitive in the future. KlöCo homed in on creating relevance in their re- and upskilling programs by providing these crucial inputs from the management team to KlöCo's HR and Learning & Development team and answering the question "What do our people really need to know?" The company made high-quality programs using different learning modalities available to all employees through its digital academy. Further, employees were entitled to participate in these courses during working hours—to make learning widely accessible and thus scaled throughout the whole organization. These efforts paid off handsomely as KlöCo transformed (and continues to do so) into a digital platform company.

Rühl finished our conversation on a cautionary note, pointing out if an employee within KlöCo doesn't want to transform themselves, there might not be much of a future for them (this maps to David Bray's "15 percent rule" we discussed earlier).

Transform or be transformed.

TWO KEY QUESTIONS

The two central questions which every company needs to ask and answer in their endeavor to re- and upskill their workforce, and thus prepare itself for the future, are about relevancy ("What do your people really have to know?") and scale ("How do you scale learning across the organization?").

The answer to the first question is a crucial responsibility of management; together with defining the company's direction, management must determine the critical skills and competency necessary to reach its objectives.

The response to the second question needs to be enabled and empowered by management, as it is crucial to ensure future skills and competencies are broadly available across the organization. And as Gianni Giacomelli, tasked with scaling up learning at global consultancy Genpact, points out, "When you do the math, you quickly realize you simply will never have enough money to re- and upskill everyone in the company if you rely on traditional learning tools. The only way to stay afloat is to democratize the creation and curation of knowledge, and make sure people embrace the knowledge in a non-hierarchical way. This means they shouldn't need to wait for anybody to wake them up in the morning and send them to school, but that learning becomes part of their normal workflow." Lars Hyland adds, "To be effective, learning has to be embedded into your work practices and so much closer to the flow of what you're doing."

Riaz Shah, partner and global learning leader at consulting company EY, focuses on doing just that for the 350,000 people working at EY globally. Identifying the need for continuous learning and, therefore, the necessity for the firm to continuously re- and upskill its employees, Shah went on to create a series of scaled programs with carefully curated relevancy for the firm's future needs. After returning to the firm from a sabbatical (to create a charter school, nonetheless), Shah was tasked by EY's CEO, who identified the necessity for ongoing learning due to the exponentially accelerating amount of change happening across all industries.

"With great support from the CEO, we decided to start with identifying the skills all of our people will need in the future, regardless of where they are in the world, how senior they are, or what they do day to day," Shah explained in our conversation. "We then curated content from the very best MOOCs (massive open online courses) in the world, created learning pathways for our employees, and assigned learning badges to them."

By creating specific, public, and transferable credentials (upon leaving EY an employee can take their learning badges with them to a new employer), EY turned the vague request "learn about AI" into a precise, achievable, and documented learning objective, such as "gain the AI learning badge by completing fifteen hours of carefully curated and highly specific learning content."

Through the visibility of EY's learning badges, combined with a tiered system based on learning objectives and level of expertise, EY created a powerful internal and external system for relevant, scaled learning. In the spring of 2022, EY issued more than 215,000 badges, with another 200,000 in progress. To keep the content relevant, EY taps into the wisdom of its employee base and continuously works with subject-matter experts in each area to keep the content fresh and up to date.

Bill Pasmore summarizes the question of creating relevance by first reminding us we need to customize the learning journey for our people to our organization and their opportunities. Leaders don't have the time (nor patience) to go through a program where maybe 10 percent of the learning truly applies to them, and 90 percent is mainly irrelevant. "I can't waste my time with this. I need to have a focused, customized program allowing me to learn from the people I have to learn from, as quickly as possible. And help me think about how to put that into action so we can move through the challenges ahead." Creating a bespoke, focused program is not hard. When EY launched its learning initiative, Shah's team curated existing courses and modules from the vast pool of existing on- and offline learning offerings. We are blessed to live in a world where you can learn anything, anytime, anywhere; the power is in the curation.

The whole challenge of re- and upskilling gets even more critical when one looks at the global skills gap: companies already face a "war for talent" regardless of industry or geography, a trend which, according to countless researchers, trade organizations, and government bodies, will only be getting worse in the future.

Re- and upskilling are crucial factors in ensuring an organization's success in the future. Going back to Herb Kelleher's remarks on people being the focal point of any business, it thus becomes clear people's skills are a core element of any business—in Kelleher's words, "yesterday, today, and forever." A team, bringing together a diverse, well-rounded set of skills, acts like a good jazz band—an analogy Gianni Giacomelli likes to invoke when talking about people's skills.

In a good jazz band, every musician brings in their ideas and insights (often from their networks) in the form of new, unique sounds which are then seamlessly picked up by the other band members, who start riffing. The best companies, and certainly the best edge initiatives, operate the same way. And for this to happen, people need to be more like galaxies rather than stars; the power is in the connectivity and combination, not the individual. As Riaz Shah summarized our conversation: "I think it is crucial, as an organization, to ask yourself, what are the skills of the people today, and what skills are going to be needed in the future given the jobs to be done? How will those skills change and how do we upskill?"

Once you start changing what people know, you inevitably start changing who they are; by adding skills, you change the culture. And as we know from the social sciences, you can transform individuals, yet crowds can only evolve.

TL;DR
To create an effective up- and reskilling initiative, consider the following points:

- Ensure the relevancy of your learning initiative by making it the job of the leadership team to determine the specific skills needed for the future of the enterprise.

- Make sure you scale the learning to the edges of the organization by putting systems into place and providing the time for your employees to engage in the learning materials.
- Consider cohort-based learning across the organization as a proven approach to maximizing your company's learning outcomes.

Your Turn

"The Future's So Bright, I Gotta Wear Shades"
—TIMBUK 3 (PAT MACDONALD)

You can't predict the future, but you can imagine and then create it. In the sultry autumn heat besetting Austin, Texas—on a cloudless day in October 2017 at the Conscious Capitalism CEO conference—I had dinner with a fellow speaker. A pioneer in the fast-casual restaurant segment, Ron Shaich is the founder of Panera Bread—a hugely successful, publicly traded company outperforming companies such as Starbucks or Chipotle by a wide margin.

Founded in 1984, Panera Bread is an astonishing and long-lasting success story finding itself frequently at the forefront of change. Only a few months before our dinner, Shaich had sold the company to investment firm JAB for a staggering $7.5 billion.

Over the course of a delicious, all-organic al fresco dinner under the stars, I was determined to learn how Shaich managed to build, lead, and ultimately sell his company. Shaich capped off a lively discussion with a succinct summary of his approach:

"Our approach has always been to discover today what will matter tomorrow and then to transform our company into a future that is unfolding before us."

Since that night, I show a slide with Shaich's quote as the final slide of all my presentations. Our role as leaders is indeed to discover today what will matter tomorrow by decoding the weak signals, evaluating which might turn into a strong signal and when, and preparing for upcoming state changes. We then take this insight and the future we now can clearly see and transform our company by avoiding common faults and focusing on the fixes. Or, we go all the way back to the opening of this book: focusing our gaze relentlessly on the gap instead of the obstacles.

I am not one for dogmatic cookie-cutter approaches. I don't believe in overcomplicated, complex solutions. A very healthy dose of common sense yields the best results. But, as a leader of the British Special Air Service (SAS) once remarked in a conversation over a few craft beers: "In the end, it's all common sense. Which doesn't make it common practice."

It might not be, as the young leader at Pearson so powerfully expressed, complicated, but just hard, which should not deter you from leaning into this work—as it is important, exciting, and joyful.

Let me leave you with a last thought, this one from chief innovation officer and filmmaker Alvaro Delgado Aparicio (see chapter "Key 1—First-Principles Thinking"):

"Just like love, innovation can't be forced. It is a voluntary act born from your dreams and courage."

Let's dream, disrupt disruption, and build what matters. The future is ours to create.

Acknowledgments

You have completed the easy part—reading this book. Now comes the hard (and fun) part—doing the work.

Writing this book was the easy part. The hard work was done by everyone who helped me along the way.

My deepest gratitude goes to all the amazing people I interviewed. Many you met in the book, and many more provided profound insights of their own: Alice Casiraghi, Alvaro Delgado Aparicio, Amy Radin, Andy Billings, Barak Berkowitz, Bill Pasmore, Bruce Smith, Cecilia Tham, Chris Clearfield, Chris Yeh, Christina Nesheva, Dave Friedman, Dave Goldblatt, David A. Bray, David Bell, David Siegel, George Constantinescu, Gianni Giacomelli, Gisbert Rühl, Grant Wood, Gustav Strömfelt, Hannah Tucker, Hemali Vyas, John O'Duinn, Kyle Nel, Lars Hyland, Lisa Kay Solomon, Marques Anderson, Marshall Kirkpatrick, Massimo Portincaso, Maurice Conti, Natasha Gedge, Philipp Pieper, Riaz Shah, Rick Smith, Rob Evans, Rodolfo Rosini, Ryan Merkley, Samantha Snabes, Ulrich Schmitz, Vanessa Liu, Wing Pepper, and everyone I forgot to mention. Without your insights, this book would not have happened.

To the crazy ones who signed up for the Author's Circle: your contribution means the world to me! Thank you, thank you, thank you, Alberto Vilar, Alexandra Schiffke, Alvaro Delgado Aparicio, Amy Radin, Andreas Franke, Anthony Pompliano, Anurag Phadke, Ari Franklin, Arthur Liebhardt, Billy Lynch , Brad Shorkend, Christina Nesheva, Dan Byler, Dan Lionello, Daniel Almeida Pavia, Daniel Chu, Dave Rochlin, Didem Foss, Dylan Dierking, Eden Benavides, Eli Bressert, Emmanouil Xenos, Erick Contag, Flo Mack, Francois Marier, Genia Trofimova , George Constantinescu, Greg Moyer, Gregg Rodriguez, Hao Lam, Heather Sparks, Inmaculada Ranera, Itzel Torres, Izabela Witoszko, Jane Finette, Jeffrey Broer, Jeffrey Rogers, Jennifer Cyphers, Jennifer Selby Long, Jessica Anne Heinzelman, João Cardoso, Jochen Schneider, Joerg Mugke, Johann Sprinckmoller, John Ruhrmann, Jorge Mendez, Jose (Chechu) Lasheras, Josep Castellet, Julian Sotscheck, Jutta Jakobi, Kenneth Peterson, Kevin Noble, Kristopher Aguilar, Lars Ivar Igesund, Lisa Andrews, Maria Saldarriaga, Marnix Langstraat, Marshall Kirkpatrick, Martin Korbmacher, Michael Roark, Michele Pitman, Miguel Coppel Calvo, Moh Haghighat, Natalia Peláez, Osvaldo Barbosa de Oliveira, Paul West, Pedro Ruiz, Pradip Das, Raju Nair, Rama Penta, Richard Hammond, Rick Voirin, Ron Larson, Ross Ellis, Sabine Bittmann, Siva Rajendran, Stephen Forte, Tal Goldhamer, Thomas D'Eri, Tom Hood, Troy Hickerson, Will Carey, and Yen Yang Lim.

To my beta readers, whose feedback was i-n-v-a-l-u-a-b-l-e: from the bottom of my heart, thank you, Andy Billings, Gil Forer, Kacee Johnson, Maurice Conti, Richard Hammond, and Rob Evans.

To all our clients at be radical and the many collaborators we met along the way—thank you for letting me try things out and for your generous feedback.

To my team at be radical—Mafe, Jeffrey, Julian, Hucky, and Jane: simply put, I couldn't have done it without you. I love you.

My deepest gratitude goes to Dan Hunter, my climbing buddy, for recharging my batteries (and climbing some insane mountains with me). Climb on!

Lastly, nobody is more important to me (and thus this book) than you, Jane. We are one.

Now, go and build what matters.

References

MIND THE GAP

Shaw, Bernard. 1962. *Man and Superman*. United States: Heritage Press.

1—DECODING THE FUTURE

Crews, Christian. 2015. "Killing the Official Future." *Research-Technology Management* 58 (2015): 59–60.

Hartley, L. P. 2015. *The Go-Between*. United Kingdom: Penguin Books Limited.

Ries, Eric. 2011. *The Lean Startup: How Today's Entrepreneurs Use Continuous Innovation to Create Radically Successful Businesses*. United Kingdom: Crown Business.

Schwartz, Peter. 2012. *The Art of the Long View: Planning for the Future in an Uncertain World*. United Kingdom: Crown.

1.1—THE FUTURE IS …

Ark Invest. 2020. "What is Wright's Law?" Ark Invest. Accessed September 1st, 2022. https://ark-invest.com/wrights-law.

Boehm, Barry W. 1981. *Software Engineering Economics*. United Kingdom: Prentice-Hall.

cloud. 2022. Merriam-Webster.com. Accessed September 1st, 2022. https://www.merriam-webster.com/dictionary/cloud.

Computer History Museum. n.d. "1993 | Timeline of Computer History | Computer History Museum." Accessed September 1st, 2022. https://www.computerhistory.org/timeline/1993.

Heffernan, Margaret. 2020. *Uncharted: How to Navigate the Future.* United States: Simon and Schuster.

Hemingway, Ernest. 1954. *The Sun Also Rises.* United Kingdom: Scribner.

Hoffman, David. 2013. "What Is the Cloud—By AT&T." April 9th, 2013. 6:47 min. https://www.youtube.com/watch?v=_a7hK6k-WttE.

Howe, Kenneth. 1996. "AT&T Drops PersonaLink In Blow To General Magic." SFGATE. July 12th, 1996.

Intel. 2022. "Cramming More Components onto Integrated Circuits." Accessed September 1st, 2022. https://www.intel.com/content/www/us/en/history/virtual-vault/articles/moores-law.

Kelly, Kevin. 2017. *The Inevitable: Understanding the 12 Technological Forces That Will Shape Our Future.* United Kingdom: Penguin Publishing Group.

Nagy, Béla, J. Doyne Farmer, Quan M. Bui, and Jessika E. Trancik. 2012. "Statistical Basis for Predicting Technological Progress." SFI WORKING PAPER: 2012-07-008.

WIRED. 2018. "The Original WIRED Manifesto." *WIRED.* September 18th, 2018. https://www.wired.com/story/original-wired-manifesto.

1.2—WEAK SIGNAL DETECTION

Braudel, Fernand. 1995. *A History of Civilizations.* United States: Penguin Publishing Group.

Clarke, Arthur C. 2013. *Profiles of the Future.* United Kingdom: Orion.

@foone. 2020. "It's a surprisingly complicated chip. You might think it's very limited because it's only got 64 bytes of ram, but it's actually using a pipelined architecture to operate at 1 instruction per cycle, giving it quite good performance for a 4mhz CPU." Twitter. September 3rd, 2020, 8:44 pm.

The VirtuLab. 2022. "What Is Amara's Law and Why It's More Important Now than Ever." The VirtuLab. Accessed September 1st, 2022. https://thevirtulab.com/what-is-amaras-law.

1.3—STRONG SIGNAL SPOTTING

Barrett, Brian. 2009. "Worst Gadgets Gallery." Gizmodo. December 23rd, 2009. https://gizmodo.com/worst-gadgets-gallery-5431759.

Brooks, Rodney. 2018. "The Rodney Brooks Rules for Predicting a Technology's Commercial Success." IEEE Spectrum. October 25th, 2018. https://spectrum.ieee.org/the-rodney-brooks-rules-for-predicting-a-technologys-commercial-success.

Elmer-Dewitt, Philip. 2008. "The Unfiltered Steve Jobs." *Fortune.* March 6th, 2008. https://fortune.com/2008/03/06/the-unfiltered-steve-jobs.

Hoffman, Reid, and Chris Yeh. 2018. *Blitzscaling: The Lightning-Fast Path to Building Massively Valuable Companies.* United States: Crown.

Moore, Geoffrey A. 2015. *Zone to Win: Organizing to Compete in an Age of Disruption.* United States: Diversion Books.

Mossberg, Walter S. 2000. "CueCat Fails to Meet Its Promise of Being Convenient and Useful." *Wall Street Journal.* October 12th, 2000. https://www.wsj.com/articles/SB971305166620370724.

Museum of Failure. 2022. "CueCat." Museum of Failure's Collection. Accessed September 1st, 2022. https://collection.museumoffailure.com/cuecat.

2—DISRUPTING THE FUTURE

Christensen, Clayton M. 2015. *The Innovator's Dilemma: When New Technologies Cause Great Firms to Fail.* United States: Harvard Business Review Press.

Gara, Antoine. 2018. "Jorge Paulo Lemann Says Era of Disruption in Consumer Brands Caught 3G Capital by Surprise." Forbes. April 30th, 2018. https://www.forbes.com/sites/antoinegara/2018/04/30/jorge-paulo-lemann-says-era-of-disruption-in-consumer-brands-caught-3g-capital-by-surprise.

Goodreads. 2022. "Search Results for Disruption." Goodreads. Accessed September 1st, 2022. https://www.goodreads.com/search?utf8=%E2%9C%93&q=disruption&search%5C_type=books&search%5Bfield%5D=title.

Google. 2022. "Disruption—Google Search." Google Inc. Accessed September 1st, 2022. https://www.google.com/search?q=disruption.

Google Trends. 2022. "Google Trends: Disruption." Google Inc. Accessed September 1st, 2022. https://trends.google.com/trends/explore?date=all&geo=DE&q=disruption.

Listen Notes. 2022. "Disruption in Podcasts." Listen Notes. Accessed September 1st, 2022. https://www.listennotes.com/search/?q=disruption.

MIT. 2022. "Why 95% of New Products Miss the Mark (And How Yours Can Avoid the Same Fate)." MIT. Accessed September 1st, 2022. https://professionalprograms.mit.edu/why-95-of-new-products-miss-the-mark-and-how-yours-can-avoid-the-same-fate.

Mochari, Ilan. 2016. "Why Half of the S&P 500 Companies Will Be Replaced in the Next Decade." Inc. March 23rd, 2016. https://www.inc.com/ilan-mochari/innosight-sp-500-new-companies.html.

Online Etymology Dictionary. 2022. "Disruption (n.)." Online Etymology Dictionary. Accessed September 1st, 2022. https://www.etymonline.com/word/disruption.

Startup Genome. 2022. "State of the Global Startup Economy." Startup Genome. Accessed September 1st, 2022. https://startupgenome.com/article/state-of-the-global-startup-economy.

2.1—DISRUPT DISRUPTION

Amazon Web Services. 2012. "2012 Re:Invent Day 2: Fireside Chat with Jeff Bezos & Werner Vogels." YouTube. November 29th, 2012. 41:35 min. https://www.youtube.com/watch?v=O4MtQG-RIIuA&t=267s.

Andreessen, Marc. 2011. "Why Software Is Eating the World." Andreessen Horowitz. August 20th, 2011. https://a16z.com/2011/08/20/why-software-is-eating-the-world.

Andrews, Ronald. 2022. "How Many Photos Does an Average Person Take and Retain in Albums When the Average Viewing Life of a Photo Us Less than 5 Seconds/Person?" Quora. Accessed September 1st, 2022. https://www.quora.com/How-many-photos-does-an-average-person-take-and-retain-in-albums-when-the-average-viewing-life-of-a-photo-us-less-than-5-seconds-person?share=1.

Associated Press. 2021. "World's Last Blockbuster Video Store More Popular after Netflix Show." Chicago Tribune. March 31, 2021. https://www.chicagotribune.com/entertainment/what-to-watch/ct-ent-last-blockbuster-video-store-20210331-6nhms-2go4ndldptojpmufexbk4-story.html.

Carrington, David. 2022. "How Many Photos Will Be Taken in 2020?" Mylio. Accessed September 1st, 2022. https://blog.mylio.com/how-many-photos-will-be-taken-in-2020.

Christensen, Clayton M., David S. Duncan, Taddy Hall, and Karen Dillon. 2016. *Competing Against Luck: The Story of Innovation and Customer Choice.* United States: HarperCollins.

Estrin, James. 2015. "Kodak's First Digital Moment." *The New York Times.* August 12th, 2015. https://archive.nytimes.com/lens. blogs.nytimes.com/2015/08/12/kodaks-first-digital-moment.

Forbes. 2007. "Nokia — One Billion Customers. Can Anyone Catch the Cellphone King?" *Forbes.* November 2007.

MSPoweruser Power. 2013. "Nokia's Stephen Elop Throwns an iPhone." YouTube. March 22nd, 2013. 1:10 min. https://www. youtube.com/watch?v=owvtKGlYFVA.

T4. 2021. "Netflix Market Share." T4. March 12th, 2021. https:// www.t4.ai/companies/netflix-market-share.

Top Video Corner. 2016. "'Nokia CEO' Ended His Speech in Tears, Saying This..| Nokia CEO Cries Out." YouTube. March 4th, 2016. 0:23 min. https://www.youtube.com/watch?v=3A6Lmy-j1QK8.

2.2—THE STATE CHANGE MODEL

Byju's. 2022. "Changing States of Matter." Byju's. Accessed September 1st, 2022. https://byjus.com/physics/changing-states-of-matter.

Company-Histories.com. 2022. "Blockbuster Inc." Company-Histories.com. Accessed September 1st, 2022. https://www.company-histories.com/Blockbuster-Inc-Company-History.html.

Kurzweil, Ray. 2001. "The Law of Accelerating Returns." Kurzweil. March 7th, 2001. https://www.kurzweilai.net/the-law-of-accelerating-returns.

Samor, Geraldo. 2018. "Jorge Paulo Lemann is a 'Terrified Dinosaur'. But he is Not Lying Down." *Negócios.* May 1st, 2018. https://braziljournal.com/jorge-paulo-lemann-is-a-terrified-dinosaur-but-he-is-not-lying-down.

Schroter, John. 2011. "Steve Jobs Introduces iPhone in 2007." You-Tube. October 8th, 2011. 10:19 min. https://www.youtube.com/watch?v=MnrJzXM7a6o.

Zippia. 2022. "Blockbuster LLC History." Accessed September 1st, 2022. https://www.zippia.com/blockbuster-llc-careers-1327661/history

2.3—THE RELEVANCE OF SUSTAINABLE RELEVANCE

Butterfield, Stewart. 2014. "We Don't Sell Saddles Here." Medium. February 17th, 2014. https://medium.com/@stewart/we-dont-sell-saddles-here-4c59524d650d.

Christensen, Clayton M. 2013. *The Innovator's Dilemma: When New Technologies Cause Great Firms to Fail.* United States: Harvard Business Review Press.

Forbes. 2007. "Nokia — One Billion Customers. Can Anyone Catch the Cellphone King?" *Forbes.* November 2007.

Hedges & Company. 2022. "Ebay.com Auto Parts and Ebay Motors Revenue." Hedges & Company. Accessed September 1st, 2022. https://hedgescompany.com/blog/tag/ebay.

Nokia. 2022. "Our History." Nokia. Accessed September 1st, 2022. https://www.nokia.com/about-us/company/our-history.

Smith, Tony. 2007. "15 Years Ago: The First Mass-Produced GSM Phone." The Register. November 9th, 2007. https://www.theregister.com/2007/11/09/ft_nokia_1011.

smugmacgeek. 2007. "Ballmer Laughs at iPhone." YouTube. September 18th, 2007. 2:22 min. https://www.youtube.com/watch?v=eywioh_Y5_U.

3.1—FAULTS (THE FOUR HORSEMEN)

Andreessen, Marc. 2007. "The Only Thing That Matters." Pmarchive. June 25th, 2007. https://fictivekin.github.io/pmarchive-jekyll/guide_to_startups_part4.

Arrington, Michael. 2010. "Overheard: Steve Jobs Says Apple Tablet 'Will Be The Most Important Thing I've Ever Done.'" TechCrunch. January 24th, 2010. https://techcrunch.com/2010/01/24/steve-jobs-tablet-most-important.

Baghai, Mehrdad., David White, and Steve Coley. 2000. *The Alchemy of Growth: Practical Insights for Building the Enduring Enterprise.* United Kingdom: Basic Books.

Christensen, Clayton M. 2013. *The Innovator's Dilemma: When New Technologies Cause Great Firms to Fail.* United States: Harvard Business Review Press.

Elliott, Edward B. 1862. *Horae Apocalypticae, Vol. I (5th ed.).* London: Seely, Jackson and Halliday.

Hargrove, Jerry. 2022. "A History of Amazon Web Services (AWS)." Accessed September 1st, 2022. https://www.awsgeek.com/AWS-History.

Johns Hopkins Medicine. 2022. "The Immune System." Accessed September 1st, 2022. https://www.hopkinsmedicine.org/health/conditions-and-diseases/the-immune-system.

Moore, Geoffrey A. 1991. *Crossing the Chasm: Marketing and Selling Technology Project.* United States: HarperCollins.

Moore, Geoffrey A. 2015. *Zone to Win: Organizing to Compete in an Age of Disruption.* United States: Diversion Books.

Nisen, Max. 2013. "Intuit Founder: 'Success Makes Companies Stupid'." Business Insider. February 26th, 2013. https://www.businessinsider.in/INTUIT-FOUNDER-Success-Makes-Companies-Stupid/articleshow/21318373.cms.

Samor, Geraldo. 2018. "Jorge Paulo Lemann Is a 'Terrified Dinosaur'. But He Is Not Lying Down." *Negócios.* May 1st,

2018. https://braziljournal.com/jorge-paulo-lemann-is-a-ter-rified-dinosaur-but-he-is-not-lying-down.

Viguerie, S. Patrick, Ned Calder, and Brian Hindo. 2021. "2021 Corporate Longevity Forecast." Innosight. May 2021. https://www.innosight.com/insight/creative-destruction.

Watson, Stephanie. 2022. "Autoimmune Diseases: Types, Symptoms, Causes, and More." Healthline. July 15th, 2022. https://www.healthline.com/health/autoimmune-disorders.

3.2—FIXES

Yahoo Finance. 2022. "EA Interactive Stock Chart." Yahoo. Accessed September 1st, 2022. https://finance.yahoo.com/chart/EA.

3.2.1—KEY 1: FIRST-PRINCIPLES THINKING

Flowers, Erik, and Rana Hannoush. 2021. "Why Every Company Should Be Doing a Follow Me Home." Intuit Developer. January 21st, 2021. https://blogs.intuit.com/blog/2021/01/21/why-every-company-should-be-doing-a-follow-me-home.

innomind. 2013. "The First Principles Method Explained by Elon Musk." YouTube. December 4th, 2013. 2:48 min. https://www.youtube.com/watch?v=NV3sBlRgzTI.

Porter, Michael E., and Nitin Nohria. 2018. "What Do CEOs Actually Do?" *Harvard Business Review.* July-August 2018. https://hbr.org/2018/07/what-do-ceos-actually-do.

VanderMeer, Jeff. 2014. *Authority.* United Kingdom: Fourth Estate.

3.2.2—KEY 2: AGILE EVERYWHERE

Agile Alliance. 2022. "What is Agile?" Agile Alliance. Accessed September 1st, 2022. https://www.agilealliance.org/agile101.

Beck, Kent, Mike Beedle, et al. 2001. "Manifesto for Agile Software Development." Manifesto for Agile Software Development. Accessed September 1st, 2022. https://agilemanifesto.org.

digital.ai. 2022. "15th Annual State of Agile Report." digital.ai. Accessed September 1st, 2022. https://digital.ai/resource-center/analyst-reports/state-of-agile-report.

Joe Justice. 2022. "Only the Best Parts—Montage by SOLJIT—Joe Justice—Agile at Tesla." YouTube. July 12th, 2022. 13:14 min. https://www.youtube.com/watch?v=XQbmMqtthSw.

Lex Clips. 2021. "Elon Musk: Dan Carlin's Hardcore History is the greatest podcast ever | Lex Fridman Podcast Clips." YouTube. December 31st, 2021. https://www.youtube.com/watch?v=4KlwNdINqeg.

Ries, Eric. 2011. *The Lean Startup: How Today's Entrepreneurs Use Continuous Innovation to Create Radically Successful Businesses.* United States: Crown Business.

Vernon, Austin. 2021. "Why Doesn't Software Show Up in Productivity?" Austin Vernon. August 10th, 2021. https://austinvernon.site/blog/softwareisprocess.html.

3.2.3—KEY 3: CORE AND EDGE

Arena, Michael J. 2018. *Adaptive Space: How GM and Other Companies are Positively Disrupting Themselves and Transforming into Agile Organizations.* United States: McGraw-Hill Education.

Brett, Jeanne, and Dashun Wang. 2020. "If You Want Creative Solutions, Keep Your Team Small." *Scientific American.* February 20th, 2020. https://blogs.scientificamerican.com/observations/if-you-want-creative-solutions-keep-your-team-small.

Christensen, Clayton M. 2022. "Disruptive Innovation." Clayton Christensen. Accessed September 1st, 2022. https://claytonchristensen.com/key-concepts.

Collins, Jim. 2001. *Good to Great: Why Some Companies Make the Leap..And Others Don't.* United States: HarperCollins.

Dweck, Carol. 2007. *Mindset: The New Psychology of Success.* United States: Ballantine Books.

Hagel John. 2020. "Unleashing Motivation for Transformation." The Deloitte Center for the Edge. Accessed September 1st, 2022. https://www2.deloitte.com/content/dam/insights/us/articles/5124_Unleashing-motivation-for-transformation/DI_Unleashing-motivation-for-transformation.pdf.

Hagel, John III, John Seely Brown, and Lang Davison. 2009. "How to Bring the Core to the Edge." *Harvard Business Review.* February 6th, 2009. https://hbr.org/2009/02/how-to-bring-the-edge-to-the-c.html.

Hoffman, Reid. 2020. "Myths About Failure." Greylock. August 20th, 2020. https://greylock.com/greymatter/reid-hoffman-myths-about-failure.

HSMAmericas. 2008. "Business of Business Is People: Herb Kelleher." YouTube. October 14th, 2008. 5:19 min. https://www.youtube.com/watch?v=oxTFA1kh1m8.

Johnson, Barry. 1992. *Polarity Management: Identifying and Managing Unsolvable Problems.* United States: Human Resource Development.

McKinsey & Company. 2009. "Enduring Ideas: The Three Horizons of Growth." McKinsey & Company. December 1st, 2009. https://www.mckinsey.com/business-functions/strategy-and-corporate-finance/our-insights/enduring-ideas-the-three-horizons-of-growth.

Tushman, Michael L. and O'Reilly, Charles A. 1996. "The ambidextrous organization: managing evolutionary and revolutionary change." *California Management Review.* 38: 1–23.

Zalik, Nir. 2010. "SodaStream to Float Stock on Wall St." Haaretz. October 20th, 2010. https://web.archive.org/web/20150610211431/http://www.haaretz.com/print-edition/business/sodastream-to-float-stock-on-wall-st-1.320137.

3.2.4—KEY 4: LEADERSHIP

Berger, Warren. 2014. *A More Beautiful Question: The Power of Inquiry to Spark Breakthrough Ideas.* United States: Bloomsbury.

Bennis, Warren and Burt Nanus. 1986. *Leaders: The Strategies for Taking Charge.* United Kingdom: Harper & Row.

Collins, Jim. 2001. *Good to Great: Why Some Companies Make the Leap...and Others Don't.* United Kingdom: HarperCollins.

Cron, Lisa. 2012 *Wired for Story: The Writer's Guide to Using Brain Science to Hook Readers from the Very First Sentence.* United States: Ten Speed Press.

Heider, Fritz, and Marianne Simmel. 1944. "An Experimental Study of Apparent Behavior." *The American Journal of Psychology* 57, no. 2 (1944): 243–59. https://doi.org/10.2307/1416950.

Hemingway, Ernest. 1954. *The Sun Also Rises.* United Kingdom: Scribner.

Hock, Dee. 1999. *Birth of the Chaordic Age.* United States: Berrett-Koehler Publishers.

Kennedy, John F. 1962. "We choose to go to the Moon." Rice University. Accessed September 1st, 2022. https://www.rice.edu/jfk-speech.

Marcec, Dan. 2018. "CEO Tenure Rates." Havard Law School Forum on Corporate Governance. February 12th, 2018. https://corpgov.law.harvard.edu/2018/02/12/ceo-tenure-rates.

Rosenthal, Sara Brin, Colin R. Twomey, Andrew T. Hartnett, Hai Shan Wu, and Iain D. Couzin. 2015. "Revealing the Hidden Networks of Interaction in Mobile Animal Groups Allows Prediction of Complex Behavioral Contagion." *Proceedings of the National Academy of Sciences of the United States of America.* Vol. 112,15 (2015): 4690–5. https://www.ncbi.nlm.nih.gov/pmc/articles/PMC4403201.